Portugal Travel Guide 2024

The Up-to-Date Manual with Easy Tips to Discover Hidden Gems, Food,Save Money, and Enjoy the Portuguese Adventures

CAROLINA EVORA

Contents

First Edition 2024

Published by Carolina Evora

Disclaimer

Hey! Before you start reading this Basic Guide there are a few things I need to share with you.

First, this is the first edition of our guide. We've worked really hard on it, but we know it can get better. If you notice anything that could be improved, please let us know! Your feedback will help us make future versions even more awesome.

Second, we had to use black and white images and maps in this book to keep it affordable and packed with info. We know it's not ideal, but we had to do it. For a better experience, check out the Kindle version. It has full-color maps and images that you can zoom in on, which is super helpful.

This guide is meant to give you all the basic info you need quickly. It's like a shortcut to help you plan your trip without spending hours online. But remember, it's just a starting point – there's always more to explore and discover on your own!

Lastly, if you like the guide or even if you think something could be better, please leave a review on Amazon. Your feedback helps us improve and helps other travelers too.

Thanks for choosing this This Country Manual! We hope it makes your trip amazing.

Introduction

This Country is an *awesome blend of old and new*. You get ancient castles, modern cities, beautiful landscapes, and friendly locals all in one place. Plus, it's one of the more affordable travel destinations in Europe. Here's why you should definitely visit:

This Country has an *amazing history* that you can see in its buildings, streets, and museums. The *delicious food and wine*, from seafood to pastries and world-famous wines, are incredible. The *beautiful beaches* offer the perfect spots for sunbathing, surfing, and swimming. And let's not forget the *warm people* who are super friendly and welcoming.

Top Cities to Visit

Lisbon

Lisbon is the *capital* and the heart of This Country. It's known for its *vibrant neighborhoods*, historic sites, and lively nightlife. You can check out the Belem Tower, ride the historic Tram 28, and explore the Alfama district with its narrow, winding streets. Don't miss the famous Pastéis de Belém – they are the best custard tarts ever!

Porto

Porto is famous for its *Port wine* and stunning views of the Douro River. Walk across the Dom Luís I Bridge, visit the Livraria Lello bookstore (it looks like something out of Harry Potter!), and take a boat tour on the river. Try some Port wine at a riverside cellar – it's a must-do!

Algarve

The Algarve is the *ultimate beach destination* with its golden sands and dramatic cliffs. Relax on Praia da Marinha, explore the caves of Benagil, and visit the charming town of Lagos. The Algarve is great for water sports like surfing and kayaking.

Madeira

Madeira is a beautiful island known for its *lush landscapes* and outdoor activities. Hike the Levada trails, visit the stunning botanical gardens, and try the local Madeira wine. Don't miss the fireworks show if you're there for New Year's Eve – it's spectacular!

Braga

Braga is one of the *oldest cities* in This Country, known for its religious heritage and beautiful architecture. Visit the Bom Jesus do Monte sanctuary, explore the historic city center, and check out the amazing churches. If you're visiting in June, the São João Festival is a fun and colorful event you shouldn't miss.

Best Time to Visit

Spring (March to May) offers mild weather, blooming flowers, and fewer tourists. Summer (June to August) is perfect for beach lovers, but it can get crowded and hot. Autumn (September to November) has great weather and is the grape harvesting season in the wine regions. Winter (December to February) is milder than many European countries, but cooler and quieter, except for the festive season.

Is This Country Cheap or Expensive?

Compared to other Western European countries, This Country is pretty affordable. Accommodation is cheaper than in France, Spain, or Italy. You can find good deals on hotels and Airbnb. Eating out is reasonably priced; a meal at a local restaurant can cost around €10-€15. Public transport is cheap and reliable, and renting a car is also affordable, especially if you plan to explore more remote areas. Many attractions are free or inexpensive, and museum tickets and tours are usually budget-friendly.

What Travelers Need to Know

The official language is *Portuguese*, but many people speak English, especially in tourist areas. The currency is the *Euro (€)*. This Country is a *safe country*, but like anywhere, keep an eye on your belongings in crowded places. Trains and buses are great for getting between cities, and in cities, trams and metros are super handy.

Chapter 1
Essence of Portugal

Rich Culture

This Country is a captivating blend of vibrant colours, intoxicating aromas, and soul-stirring sounds that echo its rich culture and history. The culture of This Country is a beautiful symphony, composed of diverse notes that have been harmoniously woven together over time, creating a melody that resonates in the hearts of its people and its visitors alike.

One cannot appreciate his rich culture without delving into its profound historical roots. The country's history is a fascinating narrative of conquests and explorations, of resilience and innovation. This Country, once a formidable maritime nation, has a history that dates back to the Roman times. Walking through This Country's ancient cities, one can marvel at the Roman ruins in Evora, the medieval castles in Guimarães, or the Manueline-style architecture in Lisbon. Every stone, every building, every street tells a story, serving as a silent testament to the country's vibrant past.

The country is a veritable treasure trove of art, spanning from the ancient Roman mosaics to the modernist artworks of Amadeo de Souza-Cardoso. His nique artistic expression is perhaps best captured in its azulejos - the intricately designed, blue and white ceramic tiles that adorn many of its buildings. These beautiful tiles are not merely decorative elements; they narrate the history and culture, encapsulating the country's soul in their exquisite designs.

His rich culture is also deeply embedded in its music and dance. Fado, the country's traditional music genre, is a poignant expression of the Portuguese spirit - a melancholic yet beautiful melody that speaks of love, loss, and longing. Listening to a live Fado performance in a dimly lit tavern in Lisbon or Porto is an experience that tugs at the heartstrings, offering a glimpse into the Portuguese soul. The country's traditional folk dance, Rancho Folclórico, is another cultural gem - a lively and colourful spectacle that reflects This Country's regional diversity.

Portuguese cuisine is another embodiment of the country's rich culture. Portuguese food is a delightful fusion of land and sea, characterized by robust flavours and fresh ingredients. From the ubiquitous bacalhau (codfish) dishes to the delectable pastéis de nata (custard tarts), Portuguese cuisine is a gastronomic experience that tantalizes the taste buds and warms the soul. The country's wine, particularly the world-renowned Port and Madeira, further enhances this culinary experience.

This Country's rich culture is not just confined to its historical sites, art, music, dance, and cuisine. It is also reflected in its people - in their warm hospitality, their vibrant festivals, and their deep-rooted traditions. The Portuguese people, with their easygoing charm and their zest for life, are the living embodiment of their country's rich culture. They welcome visitors with open arms, eager to share the stories, traditions, and flavours that make This Country truly unique.

DIVERSE LANDSCAPES

This Country's terrain is an enchanting mosaic of contrasting landscapes, each more bewitching than the last. The country's geographical diversity is its trump card, offering a plethora of experiences that can satisfy the most discerning of travelers. From lush vineyards and sun-soaked beaches to towering mountains and sprawling plains, This Country's landscapes are as varied as they are beautiful.

On the west, This Country's coastline is a visual symphony of jagged cliffs, golden beaches, and azure waters. The Algarve, This Country's southernmost region, is a sun-seeker's paradise. Here, the Atlantic Ocean has sculpted dramatic rock formations that cradle secluded beaches, while the sun paints the sky in hues of orange and pink each evening. The coastline is a labyrinth of hidden coves and wide sandy stretches, offering both tranquility and adventure.

Venture north and the landscape changes dramatically. The Douro Valley, a UNESCO World Heritage Site, is a testament to This Country's rich viticulture. Terraced vineyards climb the steep hills, creating a mesmerizing patchwork of green and gold that stretches as far as the eye can see. The river Douro, from which the region takes its name, snakes through the valley, adding an element of serene beauty to the landscape. This is the heartland of Port wine production, where centuries-old wineries produce some of the world's finest Ports.

Inland, the landscapes of This Country are dominated by rolling plains and rugged mountains. The Alentejo region is defined by its vast open fields, dotted with cork oak trees and whitewashed villages. The rhythm of life here is unhurried, offering a glimpse into traditional Portuguese rural life. Further north, the mountain ranges of Serra da Estrela and Peneda-Gerês National Park offer a stark contrast. Here, jagged peaks reach for the sky, while emerald-green forests cloak the slopes. These areas are a haven for hikers and nature lovers, with trails revealing waterfalls, glacial valleys, and an abundance of wildlife.

This Country's landscapes also include its vibrant cities, where modernity and tradition blend seamlessly. Lisbon, sprawls across seven hills, with its cobbled streets offering panoramic views of the Tagus River and the city's pastel-colored buildings. In contrast, Porto, This Country's second city, is a charming mix of medieval relics, baroque churches, and contemporary architecture, all set against the backdrop of the Douro River.

The Azores and Madeira, the two autonomous regions of This Country, offer a completely different landscape. The Azores, an archipelago in the middle of the Atlantic, is a world of volcanic landscapes, thermal springs, and lush pastures. Madeira, on the other hand, is known for its stunning laurel forests, precipitous cliffs, and exotic flowers.

Unique Allure

The distinctive allure of This Country lies in its diversity. The country extends from the rugged mountains of the north, through the rolling plains of the center, to the sun-baked beaches of the south. Each region has its own unique character and charm, offering a myriad of experiences for travelers. The enchanting Douro Valley with its terraced vineyards and quaint quintas (wine estates), the vibrant city of Lisbon with its iconic yellow trams and picturesque cobblestone streets, and the picturesque Algarve with its stunning beaches and charming fishing villages - all contribute to the unique allure of This Country.

The country has a rich cultural heritage that is deeply rooted in its history. From the soulful fado music that echoes through the narrow streets of Lisbon to the traditional azulejos (tilework) that adorns many of the country's buildings, This Country's culture is a vibrant tapestry of traditions and customs that have been passed down through generations. These traditions, coupled with the country's warm and welcoming people, give This Country an irresistible charm that draws travelers from around the world.

The allure of This Country is further enhanced by its cuisine. Portuguese food is a delicious mix of fresh seafood, succulent meats, and flavorful vegetables, all prepared with a unique blend of spices and ingredients. Whether it's the famous bacalhau (codfish) dishes, the delectable pastéis de nata (custard tarts), or the robust wines from the Douro Valley, This Country's cuisine is a gastronomic delight that adds to the country's overall appeal.

This Country's unique allure is also reflected in its architecture. From the medieval castles and fortresses that stand as silent witnesses to the country's turbulent past, to the grand palaces and monasteries that showcase its religious and royal heritage, to the charming homes and buildings that reflect its rural traditions - This Country's architecture is a fascinating blend of styles and influences. The Manueline style, a Portuguese version of late Gothic architecture characterized by ornate detailing, is particularly noteworthy.

The unique allure of this country is encapsulated in its slower pace of life. Unlike the hustle and bustle of many other European destinations, This Country offers a more relaxed and laid-back atmosphere. Whether it's sipping a glass of port wine on a sunny terrace, strolling along a sandy beach, or exploring a historic village, This Country encourages you to slow down and savor the moment.

HISTORICAL OVERVIEW

Immersing oneself in the rich tapestry of This Country's history is akin to traversing through a grand, sprawling museum, where each room unfurls a new era, a new dynasty, a new revolution. The narrative of this enchanting land is embroidered with tales of explorers, monarchs, poets, and revolutionaries, each leaving an indelible imprint on the country's cultural and historical landscape.

The origins of This Country trace back to the early civilizations of the Iberian Peninsula, with the Lusitanians, Celts, and Romans leaving their mark. The Romans, in particular, played a significant role in shaping This Country's future, establishing a strong administrative and infrastructural framework that would persist for centuries. The fall of the Roman Empire led to the arrival of the Visigoths, who ruled until the 8th century, when the Moors from North Africa seized control.

The Moorish reign, lasting several centuries, brought about a profound transformation in This Country. The infusion of Arabic culture and knowledge enriched This Country's architecture, agriculture, and arts, the remnants of which can be seen to this day in the southern region of Algarve. However, the Reconquista, a series of campaigns by Christian states, gradually reclaimed territories from the Moors, culminating in the creation of the Kingdom of This Country in 1139.

The 15th and 16th centuries marked This Country's Age of Discoveries, a period of maritime exploration that positioned This Country as a global superpower. Visionaries like Prince Henry the Navigator and explorers such as Vasco da Gama and Ferdinand Magellan charted new territories and sea routes, extending This Country's influence to Africa, Asia, and the Americas. This era of exploration and colonization brought immense wealth and cultural diversity to This Country, the echoes of which can be seen in its architectural marvels, culinary traditions, and artistic expressions.

The tide turned in the 17th century with the loss of its Asian and African colonies, followed by a devastating earthquake in 1755 that left Lisbon in ruins. The following centuries were marked by turmoil, with the invasion by Napoleonic forces, the loss of Brazil, and a series of political upheavals leading to the establishment of the Portuguese First Republic in 1910.

The 20th century brought its own share of challenges, with the authoritarian Estado Novo regime leading This Country into a period of isolation and stagnation. The Carnation Revolution of 1974 marked a turning point, ending the dictatorship and setting This Country on the path to democracy. The country's accession to the European Union in 1986 marked a new chapter in its history, bringing economic growth and modernization.

Today, This Country stands as a testament to its resilient past, a captivating blend of old and new. From the Roman ruins of Conimbriga and the Moorish castles of Sintra to the Manueline-style Tower of Belem and the modernist architecture of Porto, every corner of This Country narrates a piece of its historical saga.

Chapter 2
Before You Go

Best Time To Visit

As the sun rises over the azure Atlantic, casting its golden glow on the rugged cliffs and sandy beaches, the allure of This Country beckons. Nestled on the Iberian Peninsula, this enchanting nation is a year-round destination. However, there are certain periods when the allure of This Country is most potent. The ideal time to visit This Country depends on the itinerary, weather preferences, and the region one intends to explore.

The peak tourist season in This Country stretches from **June to September, with July and August** being the busiest months. The sun shines bright, the skies are a brilliant blue, and the temperature hovers around a pleasant 28°C (82°F). The coastal areas, particularly the Algarve region, are brimming with tourists, all eager to bask in the sun and frolic in the crystal-clear waters. The cities of Lisbon and Porto, with their vibrant nightlife and cultural events, are also bustling during this period.

The summer season is perfect For who seek sun- soaked holidays. The long, warm days are ideal for lounging on the beaches, indulging in water sports, or exploring the coastal towns. The UNESCO World Heritage sites, historic monuments, and the vibrant flea markets are also open to visitors. However, it's worth noting that the summer months, especially August, can get quite crowded, and the prices for accommodation and flights tend to surge.

For who prefer a more serene environment, the shoulder seasons of spring (April to June) and fall (September to October) are the best times to visit This Country.

The weather is mild, the tourist crowds have thinned, and the landscape is at its most picturesque. Springtime in This Country is a riot of colors, with almond blossoms painting the countryside in shades of pink and white. The pleasant weather is perfect for hiking in the national parks or sipping wine in the vineyards of Douro Valley.

Autumn, on the other hand, is a visual treat. The vine leaves turn a fiery red, the sunsets are more dramatic, and the harvest festivals are in full swing. This is also the best time to visit the cities, as the temperatures are cooler and the streets less crowded.

Winter, from November to February, is the off-peak season in This Country. The weather can be unpredictable, with occasional rain and lower temperatures. However, this is the time when you can have the country's stunning landscapes, historic sites, and charming towns all to yourself. The winter season also sees a flurry of festive activities, with Christmas markets, New Year festivities, and the traditional Carnival celebrations adding to the charm.

Regardless of when you choose to visit, This Country's rich history, diverse landscape, and warm hospitality are sure to leave a lasting impression. Whether it's the sun-drenched beaches, the historic cities, the verdant vineyards, or the vibrant festivals, each season in This Country has its unique charm.

The best time to visit This Country is dependent on what you want to experience. If you crave the summer heat and bustling beaches, plan your trip between June and August. If you desire a peaceful getaway amidst blooming flowers or changing leaves, consider visiting in spring or autumn. And if you're a solitude seeker willing to brave the chill, winter might just be the perfect time for you. Remember, in This Country, every season has its story to tell.

What To Pack

In the heart of the Iberian Peninsula, This Country awaits you with its sun-kissed beaches, historic cities, and irresistible cuisine. To fully immerse in this vibrant culture and explore the picturesque landscapes, you must pack wisely for your experience. This section will guide you through the essentials and the specifics that you should consider while packing for your Portuguese adventure.

Firstly, clothing will be a significant part of your luggage. This Country enjoys a Mediterranean climate with hot, dry summers and mild, rainy winters. If you're visiting in the warmer months, pack lightweight, breathable clothes, such as shorts, t-shirts, and dresses, preferably in cotton or linen. Don't forget your swimwear for those refreshing dips in the Atlantic Ocean or the numerous pools scattered across the country. Conversely, if you're visiting during the cooler months, pack warmer clothing like jackets, sweaters, and jeans. However, remember that even in winter, This Country enjoys plenty of sunshine, so pack layers to adjust to the changing temperatures.

Footwear is another critical aspect to consider. This Country's historic cities are best explored on foot, which means you'll need comfortable walking shoes. If you're planning to hike the verdant hills of the Douro Valley or the dramatic cliffs of the Algarve, sturdy walking boots are a must. And of course, pack a pair of sandals or flip-flops for the beach.

Don't forget to pack a hat, sunglasses, and sunscreen, regardless of the season. The Portuguese sun can be intense, especially in the southern regions. These items will protect you from harmful UV rays and potential sunburns, ensuring a pleasant and comfortable experience.

Other essential items to carry are a reusable water bottle to stay hydrated, a camera to capture the stunning vistas, and a power adapter for your electronics. This Country uses type F plug sockets, so ensure your adapter is compatible. If you're planning to use public transportation extensively, consider packing a smaller backpack or a day bag for your daily excursions.

When it comes to toiletries, pack travel-sized essentials. However, remember that most Portuguese cities have supermarkets and pharmacies where you can find familiar brands. Pack any prescription medications in your carry-on luggage, along with a copy of the prescription in case of any questions at the customs.

Don't forget to pack a good guidebook and a Portuguese phrasebook or dictionary. While many Portuguese speak English, especially in tourist areas, having a basic understanding of key phrases will enhance your travel experience.

BUDGETING ADVICE

One of the most crucial aspects to consider is the management of your financial resources, or simply put, budgeting. A well-planned budget can make the difference between an enjoyable, worry-free vacation, and one fraught with financial stress.

To begin with, it's important to understand the general cost of living in This Country. Compared to many other European countries, This Country is relatively affordable. The cost of accommodation, meals, transportation, and attractions are generally lower. However, this doesn't mean you should head to This Country without a well-thought-out budget.

Accommodation, the largest chunk of most travel budgets, can vary greatly. Luxury resorts in the Algarve or boutique hotels in Lisbon can be quite pricey. However, there are plenty of more affordable options such as guesthouses, B&Bs, and budget hotels, particularly in less touristy areas. If you're planning a longer stay, consider renting an apartment which can be cost-effective and gives you the opportunity to save on meals.

Food is an integral part of the Portuguese experience. While dining out at high-end restaurants in tourist areas can add up, there are plenty of more affordable options. Local markets are a great place to sample fresh produce and local delicacies at a fraction of the cost. This Country is also famous for its pastelarias (pastry shops), where you can enjoy a delicious pastry and coffee for just a few euros.

Transportation is another area where you can control your spending. Public transportation in This Country is reliable and relatively inexpensive. Trains and buses connect all major cities and towns, and city metro systems are efficient and easy to navigate. If you plan to explore more remote areas, consider renting a car. While this adds an expense, it gives you the freedom to explore at your own pace.

When it comes to attractions, many of This Country's best are free or low-cost. The country's natural beauty, from the stunning beaches of the Algarve to the verdant vineyards of the Douro Valley, can be enjoyed without spending a dime. Many museums and attractions offer reduced or free admission on certain days or times.

HEALTH AND SAFETY PRECAUTIONS

It's important to bear in mind that your safety and health are paramount. This Country is a country known for its warm hospitality, rich history, and breathtaking landscapes, but as with any other travel destination, it's crucial to stay informed about health and safety precautions to ensure an enjoyable and worry-free trip.

Starting with health precautions, This Country's healthcare system is quite robust and efficient. However, it's advised to take out a comprehensive travel insurance policy that covers medical expenses, including emergency repatriation. Ensure that your routine vaccinations are up-to-date before traveling, especially for measles, mumps, and rubella (MMR), diphtheria, tetanus, and pertussis (DTaP), and influenza. Although This Country doesn't have any specific vaccination requirements, it's wise to consult with your healthcare provider about any additional vaccinations you may need based on your travel plans.

In terms of food and water safety, This Country maintains high standards. Tap water is safe to drink in most parts of the country, and food hygiene practices are largely commendable. However, it's always a good idea to stay cautious. Opt for bottled water if you're in a rural area or if the tap water's taste or smell seems off. When it comes to food, ensure it's thoroughly cooked and served hot, particularly when eating seafood - a staple in Portuguese cuisine.

This Country enjoys a Mediterranean climate, which means hot, dry summers and mild, rainy winters. If you're traveling during the summer, protect yourself from the sun. Use a high SPF sunscreen, wear protective clothing, and stay hydrated. Heatstroke and sunburn can rapidly turn a dream vacation into a nightmare.

On the safety front, This Country is considered one of the safest countries in the world. However, like anywhere else, it's not immune to crime. Pickpocketing and bag snatching are common in crowded tourist areas and public transport. Always keep an eye on your belongings, don't flash expensive items, and be wary of distractions designed to divert your attention.

If you're planning on driving, familiarize yourself with This Country's driving laws. Seatbelts are mandatory, and you must carry a valid driving license, ID, and insurance documents at all times. This Country has a strict policy on drunk driving, and fines can be hefty. The use of mobile phones while driving is also illegal.

In case of an emergency, the national emergency number in This Country is 112. This number can be dialed free of charge from any phone, including mobile phones even without a SIM card.

While This Country is generally safe, it's not uncommon for forest fires to occur, especially in the central and northern regions during the summer. Keep updated with local news and follow the advice of local authorities.

Respect local customs and traditions. This country with deep-rooted cultural values and traditions. Showing respect to these will not only ensure your safety but also enrich your travel experience.

Chapter 3
Portugal by Region

The Lush North

The North of This Country is a region that brims with history and culture. Here, ancient stone castles stand sentinel on hilltops, their battlements whispering tales of battles and bravery. Cobblestone villages, nestled in the valleys, showcase a way of life that has remained unchanged for centuries. The architecture is a blend of the traditional and the modern, with Romanesque churches standing alongside contemporary buildings, a testament to the region's rich cultural tapestry.

The region's heart is the city of Porto, the second-largest city in This Country. This vibrant city, nestled on the banks of the Douro River, is a blend of old-world charm and modern sophistication. Its historic center, a UNESCO World Heritage Site, is a labyrinth of narrow, winding streets, lined with colorful houses, charming cafes, and artisan boutiques. The city's iconic Ribeira district, with its distinctive tiled facades, is a must-visit, offering breathtaking views of the river and the city's famous Dom Luís I Bridge.

The region's gastronomy is a reflection of its lush surroundings. The fertile soil and temperate climate provide a bounty of fresh produce, from succulent olives to ripe tomatoes, which form the backbone of the local cuisine. The region is also renowned for its wines, particularly Port, a fortified wine that has been produced in the Douro Valley for centuries. A visit to one of the region's quintas, or wine estates, offers the opportunity to sample this local delicacy and learn about the intricate process of wine production.

The North is also a region of festivals and celebrations, where traditions are kept alive through music, dance, and gastronomy. From the vibrant São João Festival in Porto, featuring street parties, fireworks, and folk dances, to the more solemn Semana Santa in Braga, where the streets come alive with processions and religious ceremonies, there is always a reason to celebrate in the North.

The region's natural beauty is equally captivating. The Peneda-Gerês National Park, This Country's only national park, offers stunning landscapes of mountains, forests, and rivers, teeming with diverse flora and fauna. It's a paradise for nature enthusiasts, offering a plethora of outdoor activities, from hiking and biking to bird-watching and horseback riding.

The lush North of This Country is a captivating blend of the ancient and the modern, the traditional and the innovative, the urban and the rural. It is a region that invites exploration, promising a experience filled with discovery and delight, offering a taste of the authentic Portuguese experience.

THE SUNNY ALGARVE

Bathing in the radiant glory of the sun, the Algarve is a sparkling jewel on the southern edge of This Country. This enchanting region is an alluring tapestry of golden beaches, cerulean seas, and quaint villages, all under a sky so brilliantly blue it seems painted by an artist's hand. As you venture into this sun-drenched paradise, you will find it hard not to fall under its magical spell.

The coastline is the Algarve's crowning glory, a seemingly endless stretch of sand that glimmers in the sunlight. Each beach is a masterpiece, from the secluded coves of **Praia da Marinha** to the bustling shores of Praia da Rocha. The azure waters are a haven for swimmers, surfers, and sailors alike, their waves whispering an irresistible call to adventure. At sunset, the beaches transform into a spectacle of colors as the sun dips below the horizon, casting a golden glow over the seascape.

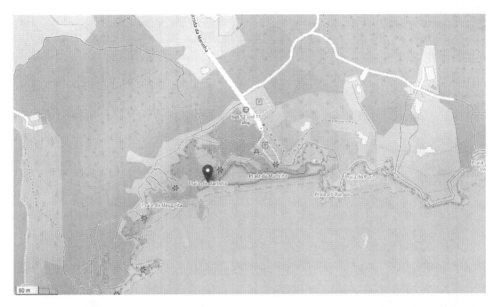

Venture inland, and the Algarve reveals a different side of its charm. The region is a patchwork of rolling hills and verdant valleys, dotted with orange groves and olive trees. The countryside is crisscrossed with trails that lead through picturesque landscapes, perfect for leisurely strolls or invigorating hikes. The Monchique Mountains offer breathtaking panoramic views of the region, their peaks often shrouded in the mist, adding an air of mystique to their beauty.

The Algarve's towns and villages are as captivating as its natural beauty. Faro, the regional capital, is a fascinating blend of historic charm and modern vibrancy. Its cobbled streets are lined with pastel-colored houses, their walls adorned with azulejos, traditional Portuguese tiles. The town's cathedral, a mishmash of Gothic and Renaissance styles, stands as a testament to Faro's rich history.

Albufeira, once a humble fishing village, is now a bustling resort town. Yet, it has held onto its old-world charm, with its whitewashed houses and narrow, winding streets. The town brims with lively bars and restaurants, their terraces filled with tourists savoring the region's delectable seafood and fine wines.

Lagos, on the western tip of the Algarve, is steeped in history. Its ancient city walls and fortresses bear witness to the region's maritime past. The town's marina is a hub of activity, with yachts bobbing in the water and seagulls soaring in the sky.

The Algarve is not just a feast for the eyes, but also for the palate. The region is renowned for its culinary delights, from succulent seafood dishes to sweet almond pastries.

The local wines, produced from sun-ripened grapes, are a perfect accompaniment to these gastronomic delights.

Madeira

Madeira, a Portuguese archipelago located in the North Atlantic Ocean, known for its year-round mild climate, rich history, and stunning natural beauty. This radiant gem, often referred to as the 'Pearl of the Atlantic', greets its visitors with a captivating blend of rugged landscapes, lush vineyards, and enchanting coastal views.

rugged coastline, adorned with black basalt cliffs. Madeira's landscapes are an artist's dream, painted with a palette of vibrant colors that change with the seasons.

The island's capital, Funchal, is a bustling city that combines modernity with tradition. Explore its charming old town, where narrow cobbled streets are lined with carefully restored fishermen's houses, their facades adorned with colorful murals. The city's heart beats in its central market, the Mercado dos Lavradores, where locals sell a bounty of fresh fruits, vegetables, fish and flowers, their stalls a kaleidoscope of color and scent. Don't miss a visit to the Sao Lourenco Palace, a magnificent 16th-century fortress that serves as the official residence of the island's president.

Madeira's natural beauty is not limited to its landscapes. The island is home to a rich biodiversity, with unique flora and fauna that have adapted to its varied ecosystems. Explore the Laurissilva Forest, a UNESCO World Heritage site that houses a vast array of endemic species. The forest's ancient trees create a mystical atmosphere, their gnarled roots forming a dense network on the forest floor, their canopies filtering the sunlight to create a play of light and shadow.

The island's coastal areas offer a different kind of beauty. From the charming fishing village of Camara de Lobos, with its brightly painted boats, to the dramatic cliffs of Cabo Girao, the highest sea cliff in Europe, the island's coastline provides breathtaking views at every turn. Madeira's beaches may not be abundant, but they are unique, their volcanic black sand creating a striking contrast with the turquoise sea.

Madeira's culinary scene is as rich as its landscapes. The island's fertile soil and abundant sea provide a bounty of fresh ingredients that local chefs turn into delicious dishes. Don't miss a chance to taste the island's namesake wine, a fortified tipple that has been produced here for centuries. The wine's unique flavors, ranging from dry to sweet, are a reflection of the island's diverse micro-climates.

Madeira's cultural heritage is deeply rooted in its history. From traditional folk dances and music to religious festivals and carnivals, the island's traditions are a testament to its resilience and adaptability. The Madeirans' warm hospitality, their joie de vivre and their love for their island are infectious, making every visitor feel at home.

The Azores

Suspended in the vast expanse of the Atlantic Ocean, a constellation of nine volcanic islands awaits the intrepid traveler. This is the Azores, This Country's best-kept secret, a paradise archipelago that promises an unparalleled experience of raw nature, vibrant culture, and old-world charm.

The Azores are a symphony of emerald green and sapphire blue, where lush, rolling hills meet the azure waters of the Atlantic. Each island has its unique personality, from the verdant pastures of São Miguel to the dramatic cliffs of Flores. The landscape is a wild, untamed tapestry of crater lakes, hot springs, caves, and waterfalls that will leave you breathless with their sheer beauty.

The islands' volcanic origin is evident in the geothermal pools of Furnas on São Miguel Island, where you can luxuriate in warm, mineral-rich waters surrounded by nature's splendor. Take a leisurely hike along the rim of Sete Cidades, a twin lake nestled in the heart of a dormant volcano. Here, the panorama of the blue and green lakes, separated by a narrow bridge and surrounded by lush forest, is a sight to behold.

Pico Island, distinguished by This Country's highest mountain, Mount Pico, is a paradise for adventurers. The challenge of ascending its volcanic peak is rewarded with panoramic views of the surrounding islands. Afterwards, descend to the vineyards of the island, where vines grow in the black volcanic soil, producing distinctive wines savored by connoisseurs worldwide.

The Azores are also a haven for wildlife enthusiasts. The surrounding waters teem with dolphins, whales, and a myriad of seabirds. Venture on a whale-watching tour, where you can observe these majestic creatures in their natural habitat. On land, the islands are home to unique flora and fauna, some of which are found nowhere else on earth.

The culture in the Azores is as vibrant as its natural beauty. The islands are steeped in tradition, with festivals and religious celebrations playing an integral part in local life. Visit during the Holy Ghost Festival, where you can witness processions, traditional dances, and communal feasts. The islanders' hospitality is legendary, and you will be made to feel like part of the community.

The Azorean cuisine is a treat for the senses, a delightful blend of land and sea. Sample the famous 'cozido das Furnas', a stew cooked underground by volcanic heat. Relish the taste of fresh seafood, from grilled octopus to Azorean tuna steak. And don't forget to try the locally produced cheeses, wines, and pastries.

Chapter 4
Eating and Drinking in Portugal

This Country's Diverse Cuisine

As you meander through the narrow, cobblestone streets of This Country, the tantalizing aroma of freshly baked bread, simmering seafood stew, and roasting meats will undoubtedly call to your senses. The rich, diverse cuisine of this vibrant nation is as varied as its landscape, reflecting the country's history, culture, and geography in every bite.

In the northern regions, you will find hearty, robust dishes that warm you from the inside out. Here, the cuisine is heavily influenced by the cold, rugged mountains and the lush, fertile farmland. The signature dish of the North is the 'Francesinha,' a meaty sandwich smothered in a rich tomato and beer sauce, topped with a fried egg, and served with a side of crispy fries. This indulgent, comforting dish is a testament to the region's love for bold flavors and generous portions.

Moving southwards, the cuisine begins to reflect the sun- soaked coastlines and warm, Mediterranean climate. Fresh seafood is a staple in this region. The Algarve, This Country's southernmost region, is renowned for its 'Cataplana de Marisco,' a fragrant seafood stew made with clams, prawns, and chorizo, simmered in a copper pan with white wine, tomatoes, and a medley of aromatic herbs. This dish, like the region itself, is a symphony of bright, fresh flavors that evoke the salty sea breeze and the golden sands of This Country's stunning coastline.

In Lisbon you can sample 'Pastéis de Belém,' a flaky, creamy custard tart that is a beloved local delicacy. This sweet treat, with its golden, caramelized top and buttery, crisp pastry, is a delightful contrast of textures and flavors that perfectly encapsulates the city's unique blend of old-world charm and modern sophistication.

The central region of This Country, known as the Beiras, is a gastronomic treasure trove. This region is home to the 'Leitão da Bairrada,' a succulent roast suckling pig that is a must-try for meat lovers. The pig, seasoned with garlic and pepper, is slow-roasted over a wood fire until the skin is crispy and the meat is tender and juicy. This dish, with its rich, smoky flavor and melt-in-your-mouth texture, is a testament to the region's dedication to traditional cooking methods and high-quality ingredients.

Portuguese cuisine is also renowned for its wines, and no culinary experience through This Country would be complete without sampling some of the country's world-famous vintages. From the full-bodied reds of the Douro Valley to the crisp, refreshing whites of Vinho Verde, This Country's diverse wine regions offer something to suit every palate.

Best Dishes

You will find your senses delightfully assaulted by the aromatic symphony that wafts from its bustling eateries, charming cafes, and traditional tavernas. This Country's cuisine is a vibrant tapestry of flavors, textures, and colors, a testament to the country's rich history and diverse cultural influences. This chapter will take you on a gastronomic adventure, introducing you to some of the best dishes that are the pride and joy of Portuguese cuisine.

Among the constellation of Portuguese dishes, the iconic Bacalhau à Brás deserves its spot in the limelight. This dish is a masterful blend of shredded salted cod (bacalhau), onions, and thinly sliced potatoes, all bound together by scrambled eggs. Each mouthful is a harmonious fusion of flavors, the saltiness of the cod perfectly balanced by the mild sweetness of onions and the earthy flavor of potatoes. This dish is a testament to This Country's long love affair with seafood, and particularly with bacalhau, which is fondly referred to as "faithful friend" in Portuguese culinary circles.

Another must-try dish is the Cozido à Portuguesa, a hearty meat stew that is This Country's answer to the Sunday roast. This dish is a carnivore's dream, featuring an assortment of meats including pork, beef, and sausage, along with a variety of vegetables. The ingredients are slowly simmered to perfection, resulting in a dish that is warm, comforting, and deeply satisfying. Each spoonful is a celebration of This Country's agricultural bounty and its rustic culinary traditions.

Seafood lovers should not miss the opportunity to try Arroz de Marisco, a luxurious seafood rice that is This Country's take on the Spanish paella. This dish features a variety of seafood, including clams, prawns, and mussels, all simmered in a flavorful broth with rice. The result is a dish that is brimming with the flavors of the sea, a true delight for any seafood enthusiast.

A trip to This Country would not be complete without sampling its famous Pastéis de Nata, or Portuguese custard tarts. These delightful pastries feature a creamy custard center encased in a crispy, flaky pastry shell. The custard is gently spiced with cinnamon, giving it a warm, comforting flavor that perfectly complements the buttery pastry. Each bite is a little piece of heaven, making Pastéis de Nata the perfect sweet ending to any meal.

For who enjoy a good hearty soup, Caldo Verde is a must-try. This traditional Portuguese soup is made with thinly sliced kale, potatoes, and chorizo sausage. The soup is thick and comforting, with the spicy chorizo providing a delightful contrast to the mild flavors of the kale and potatoes. Caldo Verde is a staple in Portuguese households, a symbol of the country's simple, homely cuisine.

These dishes are just a glimpse of the culinary treasures that await you in This Country. Each region has its own specialties, its own unique flavors and techniques, making the exploration of Portuguese cuisine an adventure in itself.

Dining Spots

As you saunter through the cobblestone streets of This Country, an enticing aroma fills the air, telling tales of age-old recipes and culinary traditions. Each region in This Country has its unique gastronomy, from the seafood-dominated dishes of the coast to the hearty, meat-based fare in the interior. Dining in This Country is not just about satiating your hunger; it's an immersive experience that introduces you to the country's rich history and culture.

In the heart of This Country's capital, Lisbon, you'll discover a vibrant dining scene. Time seems to slow down in the old- fashioned taverns of Alfama, where you can savor traditional Portuguese dishes like bacalhau a bras (codfish with potatoes and eggs) and hearty caldo verde (kale soup). As Fado music wafts through the air, each bite transports you back in time, offering a taste of the city's history.

Just a stone's throw away, the trendy neighborhood of Bairro Alto offers a stark contrast with its modern eateries and chic bistros. Here, innovative chefs experiment with traditional recipes, creating fusion dishes that are as aesthetically pleasing as they are delicious. Pair your meal with a glass of Vinho Verde or a cocktail made with Ginjinha, a local cherry liqueur, for a memorable dining experience.

Venture north to Porto, and the gastronomic landscape shifts again. This city is famous for its Francesinha, a hearty sandwich filled with various meats and covered in melted cheese and a tomato-beer sauce. No visit to Porto is complete without sampling this local delicacy, preferably paired with a glass of Port wine, the city's namesake.

Further north, in the verdant Minho region, you'll find a cuisine heavily influenced by the land. This is the birthplace of caldo verde and vinho verde, a young, slightly effervescent wine. Dine at rustic farmhouses where meals are a communal affair, often served in generous portions meant to be shared.

In the southern region of Algarve, the scent of the sea permeates the air and the cuisine. Fresh seafood is the order of the day here, with dishes like cataplana de marisco (seafood stew) and grilled sardines taking center stage. Dine alfresco in beachfront restaurants, enjoying the fresh catch of the day while watching the sun set over the Atlantic Ocean.

The central region of Alentejo, with its rolling plains and vineyards, is known for its robust, flavorsome cuisine. Pork is a staple here, and you must try the porco preto (black pig), a local breed that yields incredibly tender and flavorful meat. Pair your meal with a glass of full-bodied Alentejano wine for a truly indulgent experience.

Dining in This Country is a culinary experience that takes you through diverse landscapes and centuries-old traditions. From bustling city eateries to tranquil countryside taverns, each dining spot offers a unique slice of Portuguese life. So, sit back, relax, and let your taste buds guide you through This Country's gastronomic delights.

HIDDEN VILLAGE TREASURES

Venturing off the beaten path, away from the bustling cities and crowded beaches, you will find the hidden treasures of This Country's villages. These small enclaves of history, culture, and tranquility are the backbone of the country, each one offering a unique glimpse into the heart of This Country.

As you meander through the winding streets of these villages, time seems to slow down. The cobblestone roads, worn smooth by centuries of foot traffic, echo with stories of the past. The houses, painted in a vibrant palette of yellows, blues, and whites, are adorned with traditional azulejos, the painted, tin-glazed tiles that are a signature of Portuguese architecture.

In the Alentejo region, the village of Monsaraz stands as a testament to This Country's rich history. Perched on a hilltop, this medieval village offers panoramic views of the surrounding vineyards and olive groves. The ancient castle, walls, and whitewashed houses have been immaculately preserved, providing a step back into the Middle Ages. As you wander through its narrow streets, the scent of fresh bread from the local bakery fills the air, enticing you to stop for a taste of traditional Portuguese cuisine.

Moving northward to the mountainous region of Serra da Estrela, the village of Piodão invites you to explore its unique charm. This schist village, with its dark stone houses and slate roofs, appears to have been sculpted from the mountains themselves. The village's rustic beauty is complemented by the lush, green landscape that surrounds it, making it a haven for nature lovers and photographers.

In the Douro Valley, the village of Provesende is a must- visit for wine enthusiasts. This village is steeped in the tradition of winemaking, with its terraced vineyards producing some of This Country's finest ports and wines. A visit to Provesende is not complete without a tasting at one of the local wineries, where you can sample the fruits of generations of viticulture.

Meanwhile, the village of Óbidos, located in the Centro region, is like a living museum. Enclosed by a fortified wall, this village has preserved its medieval character, with its narrow streets, Gothic churches, and a castle that now serves as a pousada (inn). Óbidos is also known for its cherry liqueur, ginjinha, which is served in a chocolate cup for a sweet and potent treat.

These hidden village treasures, along with countless others, offer an intimate look into This Country's soul. They embody the country's history and traditions, its gastronomy and wines, its craftsmanship and artistry. Each village has its own charm and character, inviting you to delve deeper, to explore slower, to savor the essence of This Country.

Chapter 5
Where to Stay

Luxury Hotels

These architectural marvels are not just places to rest your head after a day of sightseeing; they are destinations in their own right, providing a unique blend of rich history, stunning aesthetics, and world-class service.

One cannot possibly overlook the iconic Belmond Reid's Palace in Madeira. Perched on a cliff and overlooking the Atlantic Ocean, this hotel is a testament to timeless elegance. Its rooms, furnished with antiques and offering panoramic views of the sea, exude a sense of old-world charm. Yet, modern amenities like a Michelin-star restaurant and a world-class spa ensure that every comfort of the 21st century is at your fingertips.

Equally captivating is the Six Senses Douro Valley, an oasis of tranquility nestled in the heart of one of This Country's oldest wine regions. Here, you can wake up to the sight of vineyard-covered hills, enjoy wine tasting sessions led by expert sommeliers, or rejuvenate your senses at the wellness spa. The hotel's commitment to sustainability and local culture is evident in its farm-to-table dining experiences and the use of regional materials in its design.

In the bustling heart of Lisbon, you will find the Four Seasons Hotel Ritz Lisbon, a beacon of luxury amidst the city's vibrant energy. The hotel's rooftop fitness center offers breathtaking views of the city and the Tagus River, making your workout sessions a visual treat. Art connoisseurs will appreciate the hotel's impressive collection of contemporary Portuguese art, while food enthusiasts can indulge in the culinary delights served at its gourmet restaurant.

The Algarve region, famed for its golden beaches and world-class golf courses, is home to the Conrad Algarve. This hotel, inspired by the region's Moorish heritage, boasts an impressive façade and a palatial interior. Guests can enjoy a range of activities, from lounging by the palm-fringed pool to indulging in Mediterranean cuisine at the hotel's Michelin-star restaurant.

For a unique blend of luxury and history, the Pestana Palace Lisboa is a must-visit. Once a 19th-century palace, this hotel has been meticulously restored, preserving its original frescoes, stained glass, and ornate woodwork. Here, you can take a dip in the indoor pool, dine under the grand chandeliers of the ball-room-turned-restaurant, or simply relax in the lush gardens that surround the property.

List of Luxury Hotels

Most Rated Hotels from Travelers

Hotel Majestic

- **Price:** Starting from $350 per night
- **Street:** Avenida dos Liberdades 123, Lisbon
- **Services:** Spa, gourmet dining, limousine service
- **Nearby:** A Brasileira Café, São Jorge Castle, Chiado shopping district
- **Contact:** +351 21 123 4567
- **Website:** hotelmajesticlisboa.pt

Palace of Dreams Hotel

- **Price:** Starting from $400 per night
- **Street:** Rua das Ilusões 88, Sintra
- **Services:** Infinity pool, butler service, private balconies
- **Nearby:** Quinta da Regaleira, Sintra National Palace, local artisan markets
- **Contact:** +351 21 234 5678
- **Website:** palacedreamssintra.pt

Porto Riverside Luxe

- **Price:** Starting from $320 per night
- **Street:** Cais de Ribeira 45, Porto
- **Services:** Riverside suites, wine cellar tours, private docks
- **Nearby:** Dom Luís I Bridge, Porto Wine Cellars, Ribeira Square
- **Contact:** +351 22 456 7890
- **Website:** portoriversideluxe.pt

Algarve Oceanfront Resort

- **Price:** Starting from $380 per night
- **Street:** Praia da Luxuria, Algarve
- **Services:** Beach access, water sports, ocean view terraces
- **Nearby:** Ponta da Piedade, Lagos Marina, Algarve's beach bars
- **Contact:** +351 29 123 4567
- **Website:** algarveoceanfront.pt

Vineyard Haven

- **Price:** Starting from $370 per night
- **Street:** Quinta da Vinha, Douro Valley
- **Services:** Vineyard tours, wine tasting, farm-to-table dining
- **Nearby:** Douro River cruises, local vineyard estates, Peso da Régua town
- **Contact:** +351 25 765 4321
- **Website:** vineyardhaven.pt

Castle Hill Retreat

- **Price:** Starting from $450 per night
- **Street:** Alto de Colina, Évora
- **Services:** Historical tours, fine dining, luxury spa
- **Nearby:** Roman Temple of Évora, Chapel of Bones, Évora's main square
- **Contact:** +351 26 654 3210
- **Website:** castlehillretreat.pt

Modernista Lisbon Suites

- **Price:** Starting from $360 per night
- **Street:** Avenida Moderna 152, Lisbon
- **Services:** Modern design, smart home features, private concierge
- **Nearby:** Gulbenkian Museum, El Corte Inglés, Sete Rios Zoo
- **Contact:** +351 21 555 6789
- **Website:** modernistalisbon.pt

The Azure Beachfront

- **Price:** Starting from $340 per night
- **Street:** Avenida do Mar 99, Madeira
- **Services:** Infinity pool, seafood restaurant, spa services
- **Nearby:** Laurisilva Forest, Funchal Cathedral, Madeira Botanical Garden
- **Contact:** +351 29 876 5432
- **Website:** azurebeachfrontmadeira.pt

Azores Island Escape

- **Price:** Starting from $390 per night
- **Street:** Rua da Calma 20, São Miguel, Azores
- **Services:** Thermal springs, eco-tours, oceanic views
- **Nearby:** Furnas Valley hot springs, whale watching tours, Terra Nostra Park

- **Contact:** +351 29 654 7891
- **Website:** azoresislandescape.pt

Lisbon City Panorama

- **Price:** Starting from $420 per night
- **Street:** Rua do Panorama 300, Lisbon
- **Services:** Rooftop bar, panoramic city views, luxury suites
- **Nearby:** Amoreiras Shopping Center, Eduardo VII Park, Marquês de Pombal Square nightlife
- Contact: +351 21 678 9012
- Website: lisboncitypanorama.pt

Budget Accommodations

You may wonder where to lay your head at night. Fear not, for This Country is not just a destination for the luxury traveler. It is a haven for the budget-conscious explorer too, offering a splendid array of inexpensive accommodations that do not compromise on comfort or experience.

The first type of budget accommodation you will come across in This Country are the hostels. Nestled in the bustling city centers and the tranquil countryside alike, these hostels are more than just a place to sleep. They are social hubs, filled with like-minded travelers sharing stories and tips over communal dinners. The dormitory-style rooms are clean and comfortable, with lockers for your belongings. Many hostels also offer private rooms for a slightly higher price, if you prefer a bit more solitude. The best part? You can find a bed in one of these hostels for as little as €10-€20 a night.

For who prefer a homely touch, consider staying at a local guesthouse, known as 'pensão'. These family-run accommodations offer a unique opportunity to immerse yourself in Portuguese culture. The rooms are typically furnished in a traditional style, with antique furniture and hand-woven carpets. Breakfast is often included, featuring local delicacies like pastel de nata and bolo de arroz. Prices for a pensão vary widely, but you can generally find a room for around €30-€50 a night.

If you're traveling in a group or planning a longer stay, renting an apartment or a villa might be the most economical option. With the rise of online platforms like Airbnb, it's easy to find a range of properties all over This Country, from sleek city lofts to rustic countryside cottages. These rentals often come with a fully equipped kitchen, allowing you to save money by preparing your own meals.

Prices vary greatly depending on the location and size of the property, but you can typically find a one-bedroom apartment for around €40-€60 a night.

Camping is another budget-friendly accommodation option in This Country, especially if you're exploring the country's stunning natural parks. There are numerous campsites scattered across the country, offering basic facilities such as showers and toilets, as well as optional extras like electricity and Wi-Fi. Some campsites even have bungalows or mobile homes for rent. Prices for a camping pitch start as low as €5 per person per night.

For the truly adventurous, consider trying a 'turismo rural' or rural tourism. These accommodations are typically old farmhouses or country homes that have been converted into guesthouses. They offer a unique opportunity to experience the rural Portuguese lifestyle, complete with home-cooked meals and outdoor activities like hiking and horseback riding. Prices for a turismo rural start at around €30 per person per night.

List of Budget Hotels

Most Rated Hotels from Travelers

The Navigator's Nook

- **Price:** Starting from $60 per night
- **Street:** Rua dos Descobrimentos 33, Lisbon
- **Services:** Communal kitchen, free city maps, daily housekeeping
- **Nearby:** Jerónimos Monastery, local eateries in Belém, riverside promenade
- **Contact:** +351 21 046 2233
- **Website:** thenavigatorsnook.pt

Porto Wine Hostel

- **Price:** Beds starting from $45 per night
- **Street:** Rua do Almada 317, Porto
- **Services:** Wine-themed lounge, laundry service, free Wi-Fi
- **Nearby:** Livraria Lello, Clérigos Tower, Porto nightlife
- **Contact:** +351 22 097 1034
- **Website:** portowinehostel.pt

Algarve Surf Shack

- **Price:** Starting from $55 per night
- **Street:** Estrada da Praia 102, Lagos
- **Services:** Surfboard rentals, community events, hammocks
- **Nearby:** Praia Dona Ana, surf schools, beachside bars
- **Contact:** +351 29 824 5678
- **Website:** algarvesurfshack.pt

Sintra Mountain Retreat

- **Price:** Starting from $70 per night
- **Street:** Rua da Paz 45, Sintra
- **Services:** Guided nature walks, cozy lounge, free breakfast
- **Nearby:** Moors Castle, Sintra National Palace, hiking trails
- **Contact:** +351 21 532 1188
- **Website:** sintramountainretreat.pt

Coimbra Scholars Inn

- **Price:** Starting from $65 per night
- **Street:** Largo da Portagem 76, Coimbra
- **Services:** Book exchange, study rooms, bicycle rental
- **Nearby:** University of Coimbra, Joanina Library, Botanical Garden
- **Contact:** +351 23 456 7890
- **Website:** coimbrascholarsinn.pt

Madeira Island Lodge

- **Price:** Starting from $50 per night
- **Street:** Caminho do Lido 27, Funchal
- **Services:** Panoramic terrace, organized tours, guest kitchen
- **Nearby:** Madeira Forum Shopping, Lido Swimming Complex, seaside restaurants
- **Contact:** +351 29 700 1234
- **Website:** madeiraislandlodge.pt

Azores Green Hostel

- **Price:** Beds starting from $40 per night
- **Street:** Rua da Juventude 42, Ponta Delgada
- **Services:** Eco-friendly practices, communal living area, snorkeling gear

- **Nearby:** Ponta Delgada Marina, Gruta do Carvão, local dive shops
- **Contact:** +351 29 765 8901
- **Website:** azoresgreenhostel.pt

Evora Cultural Corner

- **Price:** Starting from $60 per night
- **Street:** Praça do Giraldo 19, Évora
- **Services:** Guided city tours, thematic rooms, communal events
- **Nearby:** Évora Cathedral, Roman Temple, local handicraft markets
- **Contact:** +351 26 834 5567
- **Website:** evoraculturalcorner.pt

Lisbon Chill-Out Rooms

- **Price:** Starting from $50 per night
- **Street:** Rua dos Anjos 21, Lisbon
- **Services:** Lounge area with beanbags, board games, social dinners
- **Nearby:** Intendente's eclectic cafes, St. George's Castle, downtown Baixa
- **Contact:** +351 21 347 3347
- **Website:** lisbonchillout.pt

Douro Backpackers

- **Price:** Beds starting from $45 per night
- **Street:** Rua da Ribeira 100, Peso da Régua
- **Services:** Vineyard hopping tours, Douro River boat trips, communal BBQ
- **Nearby:** Douro Museum, scenic wine routes, river cruises
- **Contact:** +351 25 762 3456
- **Website:** dourobackpackers.pt

Unique Local Stays

One of the best ways to immerse yourself in the local culture and lifestyle is by opting for unique local stays. These accommodations, often off the beaten track, offer a slice of local life that standard hotels simply cannot match.

Waking up to the symphony of chirping birds in a charming countryside villa, or sipping your morning coffee while overlooking the tranquil waters of the Atlantic from a cliff-side cottage. Picture yourself strolling through the verdant vineyards of a centuries-old wine estate where you are staying, or experiencing the rustic charm of a traditional Portuguese farmhouse. These are not mere fantasies, but real experiences offered by unique local stays in This Country.

This Country is known for its diverse range of accommodations, from regal palaces converted into luxury hotels to quaint bed and breakfasts that exude homely warmth. However, it is the unique local stays that truly let you experience the soul of This Country. These accommodations are often run by locals, providing you with an opportunity to interact with Portuguese people and understand their way of life. The owners of these accommodations usually take great pride in their property and are more than willing to share stories about its history and significance.

One such unique local stay is the 'Quinta', a typical Portuguese farm. These farms, scattered across the rural landscapes of This Country, offer comfortable accommodations amidst lush fields and vineyards. Staying in a Quinta not only allows you to experience rural Portuguese life but also gives you an opportunity to taste the authentic local cuisine, often made from fresh produce grown on the farm itself.

If you prefer coastal landscapes, consider staying in a 'Casa de Praia', a beach house. These accommodations, found along This Country's extensive coastline, offer stunning views of the Atlantic Ocean. Not only do you get to enjoy the sun, sand, and surf, but you also get to experience the laid-back coastal lifestyle of This Country.

For those with a taste for history and architecture, This Country has a range of 'Pousadas', historic buildings converted into accommodations. These could be anything from medieval castles to monasteries, and staying in them is like stepping back in time. The historic charm, combined with modern amenities, makes for a truly unique stay.

Another interesting accommodation option is the 'Casas na Natureza', houses in nature. These are accommodations located in This Country's stunning natural landscapes, be it the mountainous regions of the north or the serene plains of the Alentejo. Staying in these houses allows you to reconnect with nature and enjoy This Country's breathtaking natural beauty.

Opting for unique local stays not only enriches your travel experience but also contributes to the local economy. It promotes sustainable tourism by supporting local businesses and preserving local traditions and cultures.

Unique local stays in This Country offer more than just a place to rest your head. They offer an immersive experience, a chance to live like a local, and an opportunity to create memories that will last a lifetime. So, as you plan your This Country journey for 2024, consider stepping off the beaten path and choosing a unique local stay. You will not be disappointed.

List of Unique Stays

Most Rated Stays from Travelers

Lisbon Art Loft

- **Price:** Starting from $130 per night
- **Street:** Rua das Artes 15, Lisbon
- **Services:** Art workshops, in-house gallery, rooftop terrace
- **Nearby:** LX Factory, MAAT Museum, vibrant local artist scene
- **Contact:** +351 21 234 5678
- **Website:** lisbonartloft.pt

Casa do Barco

- **Price:** Starting from $150 per night
- **Street:** Cais de Aveiro 22, Aveiro
- **Services:** Boat rides, canal views, traditional architecture
- **Nearby:** Aveiro's canals, local seafood markets, Art Nouveau Museum
- **Contact:** +351 23 456 7890
- **Website:** casadobarcoaveiro.pt

Hilltop Vineyard Yurts

- **Price:** Starting from $110 per night
- **Street:** Quinta do Céu Alto, Douro Valley
- **Services:** Private yurts, vineyard tours, organic breakfast
- **Nearby:** Wine tasting, Douro River, hiking trails
- **Contact:** +351 25 678 9011
- **Website:** hilltopvineyardyurts.pt

The Tower Retreat

- **Price:** Starting from $140 per night
- **Street:** Torre de Menagem, Guimarães
- **Services:** Medieval tower suites, historic ambiance, guided tours
- **Nearby:** Guimarães Castle, historic city center, local artisan workshops
- **Contact:** +351 25 321 2345

- **Website:** thetowerretreat.pt

Madeira Mountain Haven

- **Price:** Starting from $120 per night
- **Street:** Rua das Levadas 77, Madeira
- **Services:** Mountain bungalows, guided levada walks, panoramic decks
- **Nearby:** Laurisilva forest, Pico do Arieiro, local farmers' markets
- **Contact:** +351 29 123 4567
- **Website:** madeiramountainhaven.pt

Alentejo Country Cottage

- **Price:** Starting from $100 per night
- **Street:** Herdade do Esporão, Alentejo
- **Services:** Farm stays, horse riding, traditional crafts
- **Nearby:** Esporão Winery, Évora historical sites, olive oil tastings
- **Contact:** +351 26 654 3210
- **Website:** alentejocountrycottage.pt

Sintra Storybook Chalet

- **Price:** Starting from $135 per night
- **Street:** Caminho dos Castelos, Sintra
- **Services:** Enchanted gardens, fairytale architecture, afternoon tea service
- **Nearby:** Moorish Castle, Quinta da Regaleira, Sintra mountains
- **Contact:** +351 21 555 6789
- **Website:** sintrastorybook.pt

Porto Riverfront Apartments

- **Price:** Starting from $125 per night
- **Street:** Rua das Flores 110, Porto
- **Services:** Private balconies, Porto wine welcome basket, designer decor
- **Nearby:** Douro River cruises, Ribeira Square, Porto Cathedral
- **Contact:** +351 22 201 2345
- **Website:** portoriverfrontapts.pt

Azores Lava Homes

- **Price:** Starting from $145 per night
- **Street:** Rua do Vulcão 9, Pico Island, Azores
- **Services:** Eco-friendly construction, ocean views, nature excursions
- **Nearby:** Pico Mountain, whale watching, natural swimming pools
- **Contact:** +351 29 705 1234
- **Website:** azoreslavahomes.pt

Range of Options

This Country, the captivating country on Europe's Iberian Peninsula, offers a smorgasbord of travel options that cater to all types of visitors. Whether you're a history buff, a foodie, a beach lover, or an adventure junkie, This Country has something for everyone. The range of options for exploration and enjoyment in this vibrant nation is as diverse as its landscape, which stretches from the sun-kissed beaches of Algarve to the vineyard-laden valleys of Douro.

For the history enthusiasts, This Country is a treasure trove of heritage. The country's rich past unfolds in its myriad of historical sites, from the medieval castles of Guimaraes - the birthplace of This Country, to the ancient Roman ruins of Conimbriga. The UNESCO World Heritage sites in This Country, which include the cultural landscape of Sintra, the historic center of Porto, and the Monastery of Batalha, are sure to transport you back in time.

If gastronomy is your passion, This Country will not disappoint. The country's culinary scene is a melting pot of flavors, influenced by its seafaring history and agricultural bounty. Indulge in the freshest seafood in coastal towns, savor the iconic pastel de nata (Portuguese custard tart), or sip on the world-renowned Port wine. The country's myriad of food markets, wineries, and Michelin-starred restaurants offer a range of options to satiate your taste buds.

For the beach lovers, This Country's coastline, stretching over 800 kilometers, is a paradise. The Algarve region, with its golden sands, turquoise waters, and rugged cliffs, is a beach lover's dream. Surfing enthusiasts will find their nirvana in Nazaré, home to some of the world's biggest waves. If you prefer secluded coves, the archipelagos of Madeira and the Azores offer an array of idyllic beaches.

The range of options for adventure seekers in This Country is equally impressive. Hiking trails weave through the country's diverse landscape, from the mountainous terrain of Peneda-Gerês National Park to the rolling hills of Alentejo. For the thrill-seekers, there are opportunities for skydiving in the Algarve, canyoning in Madeira, and rock climbing in the Serra da Estrela.

For those seeking a cultural immersion, This Country's cities offer a vibrant mix of tradition and modernity. Lisbon city, entices with its charming neighborhoods, historic trams, and lively nightlife. Porto, known for its stunning riverside landscape and iconic blue-tiled buildings, offers a rich cultural experience. Smaller cities like Coimbra, known for its historic university, and Evora, with its well-preserved medieval center, offer a more intimate glimpse into Portuguese culture.

For a leisurely vacation, This Country's wellness retreats offer rejuvenation amidst serene surroundings. From yoga retreats in the Algarve to thermal spas in the north, these wellness sanctuaries are perfect for unwinding and reconnecting with nature.

City Center Oasis

- **Price:** Starting from $80 per night
- **Street:** Rua dos Condes 27, Lisbon
- **Services:** Central location, rooftop terrace, modern amenities
- **Nearby:** Rossio Square, Santa Justa Lift, local tapas bars
- **Contact:** +351 21 555 0000
- **Website:** citycenteroasis.pt

Seaside Escape Hostel

- **Price:** Beds starting from $35 per night
- **Street:** Avenida do Mar 12, Cascais
- **Services:** Bunk beds, bike rentals, communal kitchen
- **Nearby:** Cascais Bay, Paula Rego House of Stories, beachfront dining
- **Contact:** +351 21 889 2345
- **Website:** seasideescapehostel.pt

Porto Wine Studios

- **Price:** Starting from $90 per night
- **Street:** Rua de São Bento 45, Vila Nova de Gaia, Porto
- **Services:** Self-catering, wine cellar discounts, stylish décor
- **Nearby:** Port wine lodges, Dom Luís I Bridge, cable car views
- **Contact:** +351 22 998 7654
- **Website:** portowinestudios.pt

Alentejo Olive Grove Suites

- **Price:** Starting from $110 per night
- **Street:** Rua da Oliveira 18, Monsaraz
- **Services:** Olive oil tastings, sunset views, tranquil environment
- **Nearby:** Monsaraz Castle, Megalithic monuments, Alqueva Lake
- **Contact:** +351 26 887 6543
- **Website:** alentejoolivegrovesuites.pt

The Bohemian Loft

- **Price:** Starting from $75 per night
- **Street:** Travessa dos Bohemios 3, Faro
- **Services:** Artsy vibe, city center location, loft-style rooms
- **Nearby:** Faro old town, marina, local craft shops
- **Contact:** +351 28 999 1234
- **Website:** thebohemianloft.pt

Minho Country Cottages

- **Price:** Starting from $95 per night
- **Street:** Largo do Minho 77, Ponte de Lima
- **Services:** Rural setting, outdoor pool, home-cooked meals
- **Nearby:** Lima River vineyards, historic town center, hiking trails
- **Contact:** +351 25 774 3456
- **Website:** minhocountrycottages.pt

Madeira Panoramic Villas

- **Price:** Starting from $150 per night
- **Street:** Caminho Panorâmico 101, Funchal
- **Services:** Private villas, infinity pools, dramatic views
- **Nearby:** Funchal Cathedral, botanical gardens, mountain cable car
- **Contact:** +351 29 112 2334
- **Website:** madeirapanoramicvillas.pt

Lagos Beachfront Hostel

- **Price:** Beds starting from $45 per night
- **Street:** Rua da Praia 34, Lagos
- **Services:** Direct beach access, surfboard rentals, group activities
- **Nearby:** Lagos Marina, Ponta da Piedade, live music bars

- **Contact:** +351 28 024 5678
- **Website:** lagosbeachfronthostel.pt

Azores Eco-Lodge

- **Price:** Starting from $100 per night
- **Street:** Rua do Eco 50, São Miguel
- **Services:** Sustainable practices, natural setting, organic gardens
- **Nearby:** Furnas hot springs, Terra Nostra Park, Gorreana Tea Plantation
- **Contact:** +351 29 855 6677
- **Website:** azoresecolodge.pt

Chapter 6
Getting Around

Public Transportation

This Country's cities, you will be greeted by the efficient and comprehensive metro systems. Lisbon's seven-colored metro lines, each named after a famous Portuguese personality, are not only a means of transport but also a cultural journey through the city's history. Porto's metro, a symbol of the city's modernity, is a harmonious blend of efficiency and aesthetics, with each station being a work of art in itself. The metros operate from early morning till late at night, making it a convenient choice for both early risers and night owls.

Riding This Country's trams is like stepping back in time. The iconic yellow trams of Lisbon, some dating back to the 1930s, meander through the city's narrow cobbled streets, offering a unique perspective of the city's architectural grandeur. Tram 28, the most famous route, is a must-try experience, taking you on a scenic journey past Lisbon's major attractions.

The bus network is extensive, reaching even the remotest corners of the country. Modern, comfortable, and reliable, the buses are an economical way to explore the diverse Portuguese landscape. The Rede Expressos, This Country's national bus service, connects all major cities and towns, while local buses provide transportation within cities and towns.

Train services, operated by Comboios de This Country, offer a delightful journey across the country's diverse landscapes. The high-speed Alfa Pendular trains connect This Country's major cities, whizzing through picturesque countryside and along stunning coastlines. For a more leisurely journey, the regional trains offer a slower pace, allowing you to soak in the beautiful scenery.

The funiculars and elevators, found in hilly cities like Lisbon and Porto, not only offer an easy way to conquer the steep slopes but also provide stunning panoramic views of the cities. The most famous among these is Lisbon's Elevador de Santa Justa, a 19th-century iron structure that offers breathtaking views of the city and the Tagus River.

No visit to This Country would be complete without a ride on the traditional boats or "barcos". In Lisbon, the boats take you across the Tagus River, offering spectacular views of the city's skyline. In Porto, the rabelo boats, once used to transport Port wine, offer cruises along the Douro River, amidst terraced vineyards and charming villages.

Public transportation is more than a means to get from one place to another. It is a journey through time, a cultural experience, and a window into the soul of the country. With each ride, you will not only reach your destination but also discover a new facet of This Country's rich history, culture, and natural beauty.

Car Rentals

Car rental services are conveniently located in the airports of major cities such as Lisbon, Porto, and Faro. These services cater to a wide range of budgets and preferences, offering vehicles from compact cars for solo travelers or couples, to spacious SUVs and vans for larger groups or families.

Renting a car in This Country is a relatively straightforward process. You will need a valid driver's license from your home country, along with an International Driving Permit if your license is not in English. Most companies also require renters to be at least 21 years old, and some may charge an additional fee for drivers under 25.

On the financial side, it's worth noting that car rental rates in This Country are generally reasonable, especially when compared to other European countries. However, prices can fluctuate depending on the season. The summer months, particularly July and August, are peak tourist season, and you can expect higher prices during this time. Conversely, you can snag some great deals if you visit during the off-peak season.

When selecting a car rental company, it's important to read the terms and conditions carefully. Pay particular attention to the fuel policy, mileage limits, and what the insurance covers. Some companies offer unlimited mileage, which can be a great option if you plan to cover a lot of ground.

As you hit the road, you'll find that This Country has a well-maintained network of highways and motorways. These roads connect the main cities and tourist spots, making it easy to travel from one destination to another. Tolls are a common feature on these highways, and most rental cars are equipped with electronic devices for automatic payment.

Chapter 6

The coastal drive from Lisbon to the Algarve is a breathtaking journey with stunning ocean views. In contrast, a drive through the Douro Valley will treat you to a panorama of terraced vineyards, quaint villages, and rolling hills.

Parking in This Country is generally straightforward, with ample parking spaces available in most towns and cities. However, in popular tourist areas and larger cities like Lisbon and Porto, finding a parking spot can be challenging, especially during peak season. It's advisable to plan your parking in advance or opt for accommodations that offer parking facilities.

Renting a car also allows you to venture off the beaten path. You can explore the lesser-known towns and villages, discover hidden beaches, or take a leisurely drive through the scenic countryside. It gives you the flexibility to adjust your itinerary as you go, stop for impromptu photo-ops, or linger at a charming café you happen to stumble upon.

Car rentals in This Country offer an unparalleled sense of freedom and flexibility, allowing you to truly make the most of your trip. With careful planning and consideration, this mode of transport can transform your Portuguese adventure into an unforgettable journey of discovery.

Walking Paths

One of the most enchanting ways to intimately engage with this picturesque landscape is by exploring the myriad walking paths. These trails offer an immersive experience, enveloping you in the country's rich tapestry of natural and cultural heritage.

The walking paths in This Country are as diverse as the land itself. They traverse through serene valleys, along rugged coastlines, across verdant vineyards, and around historic cities. Each path offers a unique perspective and a different slice of This Country's charm. Whether you are an experienced hiker craving adventure or a casual stroller seeking tranquility, This Country's walking paths cater to every taste and fitness level.

The Rota Vicentina, a network of walking trails in This Country's Alentejo region, is a haven for nature lovers. The path meanders through untouched landscapes, pristine beaches, and traditional fishing villages, offering a raw, unadulterated glimpse into This Country's rural life. As you tread along, the path envelops you in a soothing symphony of crashing waves, chirping birds, and rustling leaves, making for an incredibly therapeutic experience.

In the heart of the country, the Schist Villages Network of Trails unveils a different facet of This Country. This network of paths winds through quaint schist villages that seem frozen in time. The stone houses, narrow streets, and friendly locals evoke a sense of nostalgia and transport you back to a simpler era. Walking through these paths, you will be able to appreciate the immense cultural richness that This Country has preserved over the centuries.

The Levadas of Madeira are another highlight of This Country's walking paths. Originally built for irrigation, these narrow water channels now serve as walking paths, offering breathtaking views of Madeira's unique topography. The paths cut through lush forests, spectacular waterfalls, and panoramic viewpoints, offering an unparalleled hiking experience.

For those seeking an urban walking experience, the cobblestone streets of Lisbon and Porto offer an equally engaging encounter. These cities are brimming with history, and walking through their streets feels like flipping through the pages of a living history book. From the ancient walls of São Jorge Castle to the iconic Ribeira district, every corner unfolds a new chapter of This Country's rich past.

Walking paths in This Country are not just about the physical journey; they are about the stories, the experiences, and the connections you make along the way. They introduce you to the country's diverse flora and fauna, its rich history and culture, and its warm and welcoming people. They allow you to explore This Country at your own pace, to stop and appreciate the beauty around you, and to immerse yourself in the sights, sounds, and smells of the landscape.

The walking paths of This Country are a testament to the country's commitment to preserving its natural and cultural heritage. They are well-maintained, clearly marked, and equipped with amenities to ensure a comfortable and safe experience for all walkers. So, whether you choose to walk for a few hours or a few days, you can be assured of an unforgettable journey through This Country's enchanting landscapes.

Ticket Prices and Schedules

As the sun sets over the azure waters of the Atlantic, painting the sky in hues of pink and orange, a soft breeze carries the faint notes of Fado, This Country's soulful music, through the narrow cobbled streets. This picturesque country, with its rich history and vibrant culture, is a treasure trove of experiences waiting to be discovered. However, to truly immerse oneself in the Portuguese way of life, it is essential to master the art of navigating its transport system. This involves understanding the ticket prices and schedules for the various modes of transport available.

This Country's transportation network is comprehensive and efficient, providing seamless connections between its cities and towns. The train system, run by Comboios de This Country (CP), offers a range of ticket prices that cater to different budgets. For instance, a journey from Lisbon to Porto on the Alfa Pendular, the fastest train service, can cost between 30 to 40 Euros, depending on the class of service chosen. On the other hand, the Intercidades or long-distance city trains offer slightly cheaper fares, ranging from 20 to 30 Euros for the same journey. Train schedules are conveniently spaced throughout the day, with the first train leaving as early as 6 am and the last one around 9 pm.

For those desiring a more scenic route, the regional and interregional trains, although slower, offer an opportunity to enjoy This Country's picturesque countryside. These trains are also more economical, with ticket prices falling between 10 to 20 Euros. The schedules for these services can be less frequent, so it's advisable to plan your journey in advance.

Buses, operated by Rede Expressos, offer another affordable option for travel. A bus journey from Lisbon to Porto can cost around 19 Euros, and services run from early morning until late in the evening. Additionally, the extensive network of buses also connects smaller towns and villages that are not accessible by train.

For shorter distances within cities, trams and buses are the most popular modes of transport. In Lisbon, a single tram ticket costs 3 Euros, while a 24-hour pass covering both buses and trams costs 6.40 Euros. The iconic Tram 28, which winds its way through the city's historic quarters, operates from 7 am until 10 pm.

If you plan on exploring the charming towns of the Algarve region, the regional bus services offer the most economical option, with ticket prices as low as 3 to 5 Euros. These buses operate on a regular schedule from early morning until late evening.

For who prefer the convenience of taxis, This Country offers relatively affordable rates compared to other European countries. A typical fare within Lisbon ranges from 5 to 15 Euros, depending on the distance and time of day.

What to remember?

Accessibility Information for Travelers with Disabilities:

This Country's efforts to make transportation accessible to all have led to significant improvements. Most new and refurbished metro stations now have elevators, ramps, and wide gates for easy wheelchair access. Audiovisual information systems help visually and hearing-impaired passengers navigate stations and trains. For specific needs, CP (Comboios de This Country) offers a Special Mobility Service (Serviço de Mobilidade Especial) that can be requested up to 48 hours before travel, providing personalized assistance at train stations and on board. Key bus routes in larger cities are served by low-floor buses with dedicated wheelchair spaces, and many taxi companies have accessible vehicles, though it's best to book these in advance.

Cultural Elements in Metro Travel:

The Lisbon Metro is particularly noted for its cultural adornments. For instance, the Olaias station is celebrated for its vibrant colors and futuristic design, while Parque station features intricate tile mosaics depicting historical scenes. Art enthusiasts will appreciate the detailed work at Oriente station, where natural light illuminates themed murals and sculptures. In Porto, the São Bento train station, though not a metro, is a must-see for its breathtaking azulejo panels depicting Portuguese history. These elements transform everyday travel into a cultural exploration, enriching the commuting experience.

Navigating Bus Timetables and Fare Structures:

Bus timetables in This Country are straightforward once you're familiar with the basics. Stops display schedules showing weekdays (dias úteis), Saturdays (sábados), and Sundays/holidays (domingos e feriados). For intercity buses, the Rede Expressos website provides an English language option where you can check routes, schedules, and prices. Prices are calculated based on the journey length, with discounts available for advance purchases, students, and seniors. Local buses within cities like Lisbon and Porto use a zone system; buying a day pass (passe diário) can offer unlimited travel within specified zones, making it cost-effective for extensive exploration.

Purchasing Train Tickets:

When purchasing train tickets through the CP website, you'll find options for both domestic and international travel. Start by selecting your departure and destination stations, date, and time of travel. Early booking can secure discounts of up to 65% on certain routes, notably the Alfa Pendular (high-speed) and Intercidades (intercity) services. For regional trains, tickets are often available at a standard price without the need for advance purchase. On the website or at kiosks, look for the "Promoções" section for current deals. Physical tickets can be collected from kiosks at stations using a booking reference number.

Driving Regulations, Toll Systems, and Parking:

Foreign visitors should be aware that This Country drives on the right. Speed limits are rigorously enforced, with limits of 50 km/h in urban areas, 90 km/h on rural roads, and 120 km/h on motorways. The electronic toll collection system, Via Verde, is highly recommended for those planning extensive travel by road; it allows automatic payment of tolls via a device attached to the windshield. In urban areas, parking is often regulated by meters or designated paid parking zones, with blue lines indicating pay-to-park spaces. Always check the parking signs for hours of operation and maximum stay durations to avoid fines.

Safety Tips for Cyclists and Pedestrians:

Cycling in This Country offers a splendid way to see the country, but safety should always come first. Wearing a helmet is compulsory in rural areas and highly recommended everywhere. Bikes should be equipped with lights and reflectors for visibility. When walking, particularly in areas without sidewalks, face oncoming traffic and remain vigilant. This Country's historical districts are charming but can be treacherous for the unwary due to uneven cobblestones; sturdy footwear is advised. Always use pedestrian crossings where available, and remember that vehicles have the right of way unless signs or signals indicate otherwise.

Overview of Ridesharing Apps and Services:

This Country has embraced the convenience of ridesharing, with services like Uber, Bolt, and Free Now becoming increasingly popular in both urban and rural settings. These platforms offer a seamless way to book rides through your smartphone, providing clear pricing, route tracking, and the convenience of cashless payment. Available in Lisbon, Porto, Faro, the Algarve, and expanding into smaller towns, ridesharing can be a lifeline, especially when public transportation is sparse.

• Uber is widely used and offers a range of options from budget-friendly rides to premium services.

• Bolt tends to offer competitive pricing and often has promotions for new users.

• Free Now (formerly MyTaxi) connects users with local taxis through the app, combining the convenience of app booking with the reliability of traditional taxi services.

To use these services, download the app of your choice from the App Store or Google Play, create an account, and add your payment details. When booking, you can see the driver's rating, vehicle type, and estimated arrival time. These apps also allow you to share your ride status with friends or family for added safety.

Unique Transport Options:

Exploring This Country's cities can be as unique as the destinations themselves, thanks to a variety of quirky transport options.

• Tuk-Tuks have become a staple in Lisbon and Porto, offering personalized tours that weave through the cities' historical streets. These small, nimble vehicles can navigate areas larger vehicles cannot, providing an intimate look at the local culture. Tours can often be customized, focusing on themes like historical sites, gastronomy, or even street art.

• Segway Tours offer a modern twist on city exploration. After a brief training session, guides take you on predetermined or custom routes. Lisbon's waterfront and the architectural wonders of Porto's downtown are particularly popular on Segway.

• GoCar Tours are another innovative option, where small, GPS-guided cars narrate historical facts and stories as you drive. This self-guided experience puts you in control, allowing for spontaneous detours and discoveries.

Transportation Cards, Tourist Passes, and Discount Schemes:

To maximize convenience and savings while traveling in This Country, consider leveraging transportation cards and tourist passes.

• Lisbon's Viva Viagem Card can be topped up for use on the metro, buses, trams, and ferries. A single rechargeable card reduces the need for multiple tickets and can be purchased at any metro station.

• Porto's Andante Card works similarly, offering flexibility across metros, buses, and some trains. It's available in various time spans – from single trips to monthly passes, catering to both short-term visitors and long-term residents.

• Tourist Passes such as the Lisboa Card and Porto Card offer comprehensive benefits, including free access to public transport and discounts or free entry to museums, historical sites, and sometimes even dining and shopping discounts. These passes are designed to enhance the visitor experience by making sightseeing more accessible and affordable.

To decide which pass or card suits your needs, consider the length of your stay, planned activities, and the areas you wish to explore. Cards and passes can typically be purchased online, at major transport hubs, or tourist information centers, where staff can also provide advice on the best options for your itinerary.

Advice on Avoiding Peak Hours and Navigating Service Interruptions:

To optimize your travel experience in This Country, planning around peak transit times is advisable. Typically, urban areas experience the most congestion from 7-9 AM and 5-7 PM on weekdays, coinciding with local work commutes. Opting for travel during midday or late evening can afford a more relaxed journey, with fewer crowds and sometimes lower fares. Moreover, many cities like Lisbon and Porto feature dynamic nightlife and dining scenes that are best enjoyed without the rush.

When confronted with unexpected strikes or delays, which are not uncommon due to labor disputes or maintenance work, proactive information gathering is key. Utilize official transportation websites, mobile apps, or customer service hotlines for the latest updates. Social media platforms can also offer real-time insights and alternative recommendations from fellow travelers. Local news outlets often provide coverage of larger strikes or disruptions. Exploring alternative transportation modes, such as bicycles or electric scooters available for rent throughout major cities, can serve as both an efficient and environmentally friendly backup plan.

Spotlight on Regional Transportation Quirks or Specialties:

This Country's diverse regions offer unique transportation experiences that can become highlights of your visit. The Douro Valley's wine tours are a quintessential example, where specialized shuttle services navigate between vineyards, eliminating the need for personal transportation and allowing full immersion in the wine-tasting experience. Madeira's cable cars and traditional toboggans offer not just transit but an adventure, presenting unmatched views of the island's lush landscapes and providing a thrilling descent from Monte to Funchal. In the Azores, short, scenic flights between islands showcase the archipelago's volcanic beauty and are often the only way to access certain remote spots.

Overview of Services Catering to Eco-Friendly Travel and Accessibility:

This Country's commitment to sustainable travel is evident in its extensive offerings for eco-friendly transportation. Urban centers boast well-developed networks of cycle paths, encouraging both locals and tourists to opt for biking over car travel. Cities like Lisbon are expanding their fleets of electric buses and trams, significantly reducing urban emissions. The nationwide train network serves as a testament to the country's dedication to eco-conscious long-distance travel, with services like the Alfa Pendular providing a fast, comfortable, and greener alternative to flying or driving between major cities.

List of Hotlines and Support Centers for Travel-Related Emergencies:

Getting Around

In any travel scenario, having access to reliable emergency contact information is crucial. For comprehensive assistance:

• National Emergency Number: 112 is the go-to for immediate help across This Country, offering support in multiple languages.

• Comboios de This Country (CP) Customer Support: +351 707 210 220 is available for inquiries related to train schedules, disruptions, and services. Their website and mobile app also provide real-time updates and online ticketing options.

• Metro Lisbon Customer Service: +351 21 350 0155 can assist with everything from lost items to service schedules, ensuring a smooth metro experience in the capital.

• Porto Metro Support: +351 22 508 1000 offers detailed information on Porto's metro operations, including accessibility features and station amenities.

• Rede Expressos Customer Service: +351 707 223 344 covers This Country's extensive bus network, providing assistance with routes, timetables, and bookings for national and regional bus travel.

Chapter 7
Attractions and Activities

Top Sights

The country's top sights are a testament to its diverse heritage, ranging from ancient castles to modern architecture, verdant vineyards to sun-kissed beaches, and bustling cities to tranquil villages.

In the heart of This Country's capital, **Lisbon**, stands the majestic São Jorge Castle. Perched atop a hill, this fortress offers panoramic views of the city and the Tagus River. Its sturdy walls, dating back to the Moorish period, whisper tales of the past. Wander through the castle's lush gardens, explore its ancient towers, and immerse yourself in the historical exhibits within the Ulysses Tower.

A short distance away, the Jerónimos Monastery, a UNESCO World Heritage Site, is a testament to This Country's Age of Discovery. The ornate Manueline architecture is a sight to behold, with intricate carvings depicting maritime elements and symbols of the time. The monastery is also the resting place of the famous explorer, Vasco da Gama, adding to its historical significance.

In Porto, the Livraria Lello bookstore is a must-visit. Regarded as one of the most beautiful bookstores in the world, its neo-Gothic façade hides a stunning interior. A winding staircase, stained glass ceiling, and rows upon rows of books create a magical atmosphere that will transport any literary enthusiast into a world of imagination.

For nature lovers, the Douro Valley offers a serene escape. Rolling hills adorned with terraced vineyards stretch as far as the eye can see, creating a mesmerizing landscape. The valley is renowned for its Port wine production, and a visit wouldn't be complete without a wine tasting tour. As you sip on the region's famous wine, the serene beauty of the Douro River and its surrounding vineyards is sure to captivate you.

On the southernmost tip of This Country, the Algarve region beckons with its stunning coastline. The golden beaches are framed by towering cliffs, creating secluded coves that are perfect for a relaxing day under the sun. The turquoise waters of the Atlantic are a refreshing contrast to the warm sand, offering opportunities for swimming and snorkeling.

In the charming town of Sintra, the Pena Palace is a sight straight out of a fairytale. The colorful palace stands proudly against the backdrop of the Sintra Mountains, its unique blend of architectural styles making it a standout landmark. The surrounding park, filled with exotic plants and trees, adds to the palace's enchanting appeal.

This Country's top sights are as diverse as they are beautiful, each offering a unique glimpse into the country's soul. From the historic landmarks in Lisbon and Porto to the breathtaking landscapes of the Douro Valley and Algarve, This Country is a country that promises unforgettable experiences at every turn. Whether you're a history buff, a nature lover, or a beach bum, This Country has something for everyone. As you explore the country's top sights, you'll find yourself falling in love with its charm, its people, and its undeniable allure.

Belem Tower, Lisbon

The iconic Belem Tower, or Torre de Belem, is more than just a landmark; it's a symbol of This Country's grand Age of Exploration. Constructed between 1514 and 1520 as part of the defense system at the mouth of the Tagus River, this UNESCO World Heritage Site has also served as a lighthouse and customs house. Its architectural style is Manueline, characterized by intricate sculptures of maritime elements, reflecting This Country's naval dominance. To make the most of your visit, aim to arrive just as it opens or during the last hour before closing to avoid the crowds. The climb to the top may be narrow and steep, but the panoramic view of the Belem district and the vast Tagus River is your reward. Also, spend some time exploring the bastion's interior, where exhibitions detail the tower's history and significance in maritime exploration.

Coimbra University, Coimbra

Coimbra University isn't just a seat of learning; it's a monument to the enduring legacy of Portuguese education, holding the title as one of the oldest universities in continuous operation in the world since its founding in 1290. The university complex is a tapestry of architectural styles, with the crowning jewel being the Biblioteca Joanina, celebrated for its opulent Baroque decor. The library houses about 250,000 volumes dating from the 12th to the 18th centuries, encompassing a wide range of knowledge. To visit, you'll need to book a timed entry slot, as access is restricted to protect the ancient texts. While there, also explore the Capela de São Miguel, a chapel with impressive Baroque organ and stunning azulejos (tiles). The university's Alta and Sofia wings were designated a UNESCO World Heritage site in 2013, solidifying its importance. Don't miss the chance to wander the university's grounds for sweeping views over the city of Coimbra below.

Conímbriga Roman Ruins

Located just a few kilometers from Coimbra, the Conímbriga Roman Ruins transport visitors back to This Country's Roman past. This archaeological site, one of the best-preserved Roman ruins in the country, provides a window into ancient civilization with its extensive network of residential homes, public baths, and intricate mosaics that have stood the test of time. The highlight is the House of Fountains, a residential complex adorned with elaborate mosaics and an intricate water feature system. A visit to the on-site museum enriches the experience, displaying artifacts that have been unearthed, from coins to surgical tools, painting a vivid picture of daily life in Roman Conímbriga. The ruins are extensive, so allocate at least half a day to fully appreciate this historical treasure. Comfortable footwear is a must as the terrain can be uneven, and consider bringing a hat and water during summer months as shade is limited.

Hidden Gems

In the northern region, tucked away amid the verdant green hills of Minho, sits the charming town of Ponte de Lima. It's a place where time seems to have stood still, with its medieval bridge, quaint houses and the serene Lima River flowing gently by. The town is also known for its vinho verde, a unique green wine that is as refreshing as the surroundings. A visit to Ponte de Lima is like stepping into a time capsule, offering a glimpse into This Country's past.

Moving southward, nestled amid the rugged cliffs of the Alentejo coastline, lies the picturesque village of Zambujeira do Mar. Although it's known for its breathtaking views of the Atlantic Ocean, it's the annual summer music festival that really puts this village on the map. The festival, known as Festival do Sudoeste, attracts music lovers from across the globe, making this tranquil seaside haven a vibrant cultural hotspot.

Attractions and Activities

In the heart of This Country, hidden within the lush forests of the Serra da Estrela mountain range, is the enchanting village of Piódão. This secluded hamlet, with its slate-roofed houses and winding cobblestone streets, is a sight to behold. The beauty of Piódão lies in its simplicity and the warmth of its people, making it a must-visit destination for those seeking an authentic Portuguese experience.

The Lisbon City despite being a bustling metropolis, also holds its own share of hidden gems. Venture off the beaten track and you'll discover the enchanting neighbourhood of Mouraria. Known as the birthplace of Fado music, this vibrant district is a melting pot of cultures, colours and flavours. The narrow, winding streets are lined with tiny Fado bars, colourful murals and small eateries serving delicious local cuisine.

In the southernmost region of the Algarve, away from the crowded beaches and tourist resorts, you'll find the tranquil Ria Formosa Natural Park. This unique coastal lagoon, with its diverse wildlife and pristine beaches, is a paradise for nature lovers. Whether you choose to explore the park by boat, by bike or on foot, the beauty of Ria Formosa will leave you spellbound.

These are just a few of the hidden gems that This Country has to offer. Each one is unique, each one has a story to tell, and each one is waiting to be discovered. So, as you plan your trip to This Country, remember to venture off the beaten path. You never know what treasures you might find.

Monsaraz

Monsaraz is a captivating medieval village nestled in the heart of the Alentejo region, offering visitors a tranquil retreat into history and nature. Perched high on a hill, this fortified village is surrounded by ancient walls that have protected its timeless charm for centuries. As you wander through its cobbled lanes, you'll be greeted by beautifully preserved whitewashed houses, traditional handicraft shops selling local pottery and textiles, and intimate wine bars offering tastings of the region's renowned wines.

The village's main attraction, aside from its breathtaking views of the sprawling Alqueva Dam and the rolling hills of Alentejo, is the imposing castle at Monsaraz's highest point. The castle's battlements provide a panoramic viewpoint that is especially magical at sunset. For history enthusiasts, the nearby megalithic sites, including the Cromlech of Xerez, offer a deeper dive into the region's ancient past. Monsaraz's blend of historical significance, natural beauty, and serene atmosphere makes it a must-visit for those seeking to uncover the Alentejo's hidden treasures.

Nazaré

Nazaré, once a quaint fishing village on This Country's Silver Coast, has transformed into a world-renowned surfing destination, famous for its colossal waves that crash onto Praia do Norte. These waves, often reaching heights of over 30 meters, have put Nazaré on the map for thrill-seekers and surf enthusiasts from across the globe. Beyond the surf, Nazaré retains its traditional charm with a lively promenade lined with seafood restaurants serving fresh catches of the day, colorful boats dotting the shoreline, and locals donning traditional attire, including the iconic seven skirts.

The village is divided into three main districts: Praia (the beachfront), Pederneira, and Sítio, located atop a cliff accessible by a funicular railway. Sítio offers stunning views of the bay and is home to the Sanctuary of Our Lady of Nazaré, a pilgrimage site with a legend that dates back to the 12th century. Whether you're there to catch the waves, soak in the rich culture, or simply enjoy the stunning seaside views, Nazaré offers a vibrant mix of natural wonder and cultural depth.

Schist Villages

The Schist Villages of central This Country are a hidden network of 27 stone villages that seem to emerge naturally from the landscape itself. These villages, built from the dark schist rock that dominates the region, are characterized by their slate-roofed houses, winding streets, and an ambiance of peaceful seclusion. Embedded within the lush forests and rugged mountains of central This Country, the villages are interconnected by a series of hiking and biking trails that invite exploration of the stunning natural surroundings and the traditional Portuguese rural lifestyle.

Outdoor Adventures

This Country, a splendid gem on the Iberian Peninsula, is a haven for outdoor enthusiasts. Its diverse landscapes - from the sun-kissed, golden beaches of the Algarve to the verdant rolling hills of the Douro Valley and the rugged peaks of the Serra da Estrela - provide a stunning backdrop for a plethora of outdoor adventures.

Experience along the coastline, where the Atlantic Ocean has sculpted a play-ground for surfers. The coast of This Country, particularly the Algarve and the area around Peniche, is renowned for its powerful swells and consistent waves, attracting surfers from around the globe. Beginners can find numerous surf schools dotting the coast, while experienced surfers can tackle the world-class waves at spots like Praia do Norte in Nazaré, famous for its record-breaking waves.

For a slice of tranquillity, head inland to the Douro Valley, a UNESCO World Heritage site. Here, the undulating terraces of vineyards create a mesmerizing patchwork of greens and golds, interrupted only by the serpentine river that winds its way through the valley. The area is perfect for hiking or cycling, with numerous trails offering stunning panoramic views. Alternatively, take a leisurely boat trip down the river and marvel at the spectacular scenery while sipping on some world-class port wine.

If you're a wildlife enthusiast, head to the Ria Formosa Natural Park in the Algarve. This unique coastal lagoon system is a paradise for bird watchers, with more than 200 different species of birds visiting throughout the year. Hike or cycle through the park's trails, or kayak through the lagoon's channels, keeping your eyes peeled for flamingos, spoonbills, and the rare purple swamphen.

Further north, the Peneda-Gerês National Park, This Country's only national park, offers a wealth of outdoor activities. Hike through its rugged landscapes, where ancient stone villages blend seamlessly into the natural surroundings. Look out for wild Garrano horses grazing on the hillsides, and soak in the therapeutic waters of the natural hot springs at the park's heart.

For the more adventurous, the Serra da Estrela, This Country's highest mountain range, is a must-visit. In winter, its snow-covered peaks offer the best skiing and snowboarding in the country. In summer, its glacial valleys, clear rivers, and majestic waterfalls transform into ideal locations for hiking, mountain biking, and wild swimming.

Don't miss the chance to explore This Country's underwater world. The country's coastline is dotted with excellent dive sites, from underwater caves in the Algarve to shipwrecks off the coast of Lisbon. The Arrábida Marine Park, with its crystal-clear waters and abundant marine life, is a particular highlight for divers and snorkelers.

Whale and Dolphin Watching in the Azores

The Azores Archipelago serves as a prime location for encountering whales and dolphins in their natural oceanic habitat. The deep waters surrounding these volcanic islands are a haven for marine life, making them an ideal spot for whale and dolphin watching. From the gentle giants like the blue and fin whales to the playful pods of dolphins, including common and Atlantic spotted dolphins, the diversity is astounding. Most boat tours operate out of São Miguel, Pico, and Faial islands, offering half-day or full-day excursions led by marine biologists. These experts share insights about the behaviors and conservation of these magnificent creatures, enhancing your experience. The peak season runs from April to October when the weather is favorable, and the sea is teeming with life. Essential tips for this adventure include dressing in layers, as temperatures can vary, and bringing binoculars for a closer look from the boat. Most importantly, these tours are committed to the respectful observation of wildlife, ensuring minimal disturbance to the animals.

Via Algarviana

Spanning the breadth of This Country's Algarve region, the Via Algarviana trail unveils the hidden interior of this popular tourist destination. Stretching over 300 kilometers from Alcoutim in the east to Cape St. Vincent in the west, this trail diverges from the bustling coastal resorts, offering a peaceful journey through the heart of the Algarve. The route is segmented into manageable stages, making it accessible for day hikers or those looking to embark on the entire trek. Along the way, hikers traverse through traditional villages, past historic monuments, and across diverse landscapes, from fragrant orange groves to dense cork oak forests. The trail is well-marked, with detailed maps available, ensuring a safe and enjoyable experience. Spring, with its wildflower blooms, and autumn, offering cooler temperatures and softer light, are the ideal seasons for tackling the Via Algarviana. Preparation is key; sturdy hiking boots, plenty of water, and a good map are essentials. For the intrepid explorer, the Via Algarviana is a gateway to the Algarve's lesser-known wonders.

Kayaking in the Alentejo

Kayaking through the Alentejo's waterways offers a serene and intimate connection with the region's untouched landscapes. The rivers Mira and Guadiana, among others, serve as picturesque routes, meandering through the Alentejo's varied terrain, from lush riverine ecosystems to dramatic cliff-lined coasts. These kayaking journeys allow for an up-close exploration of the area's biodiversity, with opportunities to spot endemic bird species, riverine flora, and perhaps the elusive otter. Kayaking tours cater to all experience levels, providing options from leisurely paddles in calm waters to more exhilarating routes that challenge and engage. Operators often include ecological and historical commentary, enriching the paddling experience with stories of the region's past and present. For those seeking solitude, self-guided routes offer the freedom to explore at one's own pace. Regardless of the chosen path, safety considerations are paramount; wearing life jackets and being mindful of weather conditions ensure a safe and memorable adventure. As the sun sets, casting golden hues over the tranquil waters, kayaking in the Alentejo becomes an unforgettable way to witness the natural beauty of one of This Country's most cherished regions.

Cultural Explorations

This Country, a country rich in culture and history, is a treasure trove waiting to be explored. The vibrant culture of This Country is a harmonious blend of tradition and modernity, making it an ideal destination for cultural explorations. The Portuguese culture is deeply rooted in the past, with influences from the Romans, Moors, and Christians, which are reflected in their art, architecture, music, and cuisine.

The city is a cultural canvas, with its charming old quarters, cobblestone streets, and iconic yellow trams. Here, you can explore the UNESCO World Heritage site, the Jerónimos Monastery, a prime example of Manueline architecture. Nearby, there's the **Torre de Belém**, a 16th-century tower with a stunning view of the sea. These structures are a testament to This Country's Age of Discoveries and are a must-visit for history enthusiasts.

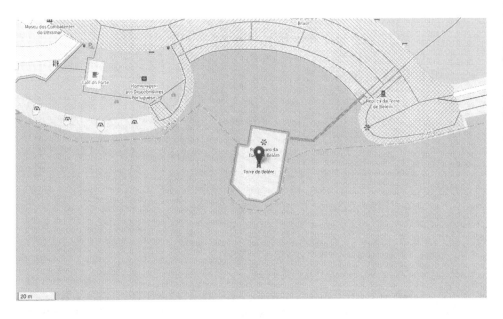

This Country's rich history is also reflected in its music, particularly Fado. This soulful music genre, recognized by UNESCO as a World Intangible Cultural Heritage, is a poignant expression of the Portuguese soul. Listening to the melancholic tunes of Fado in the old quarters of Alfama or Mouraria is an experience that will touch your heart and give you a deeper understanding of the Portuguese spirit.

Another fascinating aspect of Portuguese culture is its cuisine, known for its diversity and richness. The Portuguese gastronomy is influenced by the sea, with dishes like Bacalhau (codfish), Polvo à lagareiro (octopus), and Caldeirada (fish stew) taking center stage. Pastel de Nata, a creamy egg tart, is a signature sweet treat you can't miss. A visit to the local markets, such as the Mercado da Ribeira in Lisbon or Mercado do Bolhão in Porto, will give you a taste of the fresh local produce and the warm hospitality of the Portuguese people.

This Country's culture is also evident in its festivals. From the lively Carnival of Madeira and the Festa de São João in Porto to the Holy Week in Braga, these festivals offer a glimpse into the local traditions and customs. They are filled with music, dance, processions, and food, making them a vibrant and colorful spectacle.

The country is also home to a rich selection of museums and galleries. The Museu Calouste Gulbenkian in Lisbon houses a diverse collection of art from around the world, while the Museu de Arte Contemporânea in Porto is a haven for modern art lovers. The Museu Nacional do Azulejo, dedicated to the traditional tilework of This Country, is a unique cultural attraction.

This Country's cultural experience extends to its charming towns and villages. Sintra, a UNESCO World Heritage site, is known for its romantic palaces and lush gardens. Óbidos, a medieval town, transports you back in time with its narrow cobbled streets and fortified walls.

Port Wine Cellars in Vila Nova de Gaia

Vila Nova de Gaia is the go-to spot for learning about and tasting This Country's famous Port wine. Here, along the Douro River, hundreds of barrels age in cool, dark cellars. A visit here is a journey through history, where you'll discover how Port wine became a global favorite. Starting in the 17th century, winemakers added grape spirit to wine to stop fermentation, creating a sweeter, stronger drink that sailors could take on long voyages.

Walking through a cellar, you'll see rows upon rows of barrels and learn about the aging process that gives Port wine its rich flavors. Tours often end with a chance to try different Ports, helping you understand the differences between Ruby, Tawny, and Vintage varieties. Some famous cellars like Sandeman and Taylor's offer not just tastings but also workshops where you can dive deeper into Port wine knowledge. It's smart to book your spot ahead of time, especially if you're visiting during busy months.

Traditional Fado Houses in Alfama, Lisbon

Fado is the music of This Country's soul, filled with emotion and depth. The best place to experience it is in Alfama, Lisbon's oldest neighborhood. Here, small, cozy Fado houses offer live performances that tug at the heartstrings. Listening to Fado, you'll feel the saudade, a sense of longing and nostalgia, that's central to Portuguese culture.

Places like Casa de Linhares and Clube de Fado in Alfama welcome you with warm, inviting atmospheres where music fills the air. These spots often serve delicious Portuguese dishes, making for a perfect evening of culture and cuisine. To ensure you get a seat, make a reservation before you go. A night of Fado is unforgettable, connecting you to the stories and emotions of This Country through song.

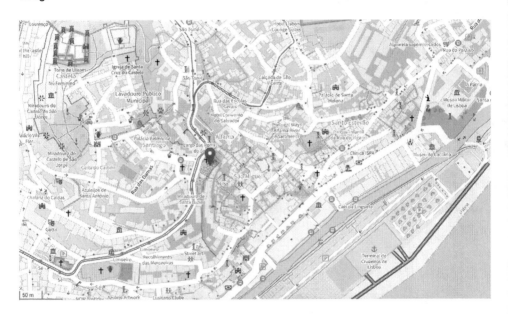

Portuguese Tile-Making Workshops

Azulejos, or ceramic tiles, are a beautiful part of Portuguese art, seen on buildings across the country. These tiles are not just decoration; they tell stories and preserve history. In Lisbon and Porto, you can find workshops that teach you how to make these tiles. It's a fun, hands-on way to connect with Portuguese culture and create your own piece of art to take home.

In a workshop, you'll learn the steps of tile-making, from designing your pattern to painting and glazing. Studios like Viúva Lamego in Lisbon offer sessions for all skill levels, guided by experienced artists. You'll leave not just with a tile but with a deeper appreciation for this traditional art form. Booking in advance is recommended, as these workshops offer personalized experiences in small groups.

Culinary Experience:

Food Markets

Time Out Market in Lisbon isn't just a market; it's a culinary showcase where some of the city's best chefs and restaurants serve up their signature dishes. It's like visiting dozens of restaurants at once, all under one roof. From traditional bacalhau (codfish) dishes to innovative cuisine, it's a place to explore a wide array of Portuguese flavors. The vibrant atmosphere, combined with communal seating, makes for a lively dining experience where you can chat with locals and fellow travelers.

Mercado do Bolhão in Porto offers a more traditional market experience, with its lively vendors selling everything from fresh fruit and vegetables to fish, meat, and flowers. This market is a feast for the senses, with the colors, smells, and sounds creating a vivid snapshot of Portuguese daily life. Taking a stroll through Bolhão is not just about shopping; it's about feeling the pulse of the city, discovering local specialties, and maybe even catching a cooking tip or two from the friendly stall-holders.

Other cities like Coimbra, with its Mercado Municipal D. Pedro V, also boast vibrant food markets where you can sample fresh, local produce and traditional snacks. These markets are integral to the community, serving as meeting places where culture and cuisine mingle.

Lisbon

- **Time Out Market Lisboa**
- **Location**: Avenida 24 de Julho, Mercado da Ribeira, Cais do Sodré, Lisbon
- **Highlights**: A curated mix of Lisbon's best foods, from traditional dishes to contemporary cuisine.
- **Info**: Open daily, this market offers a wide selection of food stalls, restaurants, and bars under one roof, showcasing the diversity of Portuguese gastronomy.
- **Mercado** de Campo de Ourique
- **Location**: Rua Coelho da Rocha, Campo de Ourique, Lisbon
- **Highlights**: A neighborhood market offering fresh produce, meats, fish, and a variety of ready-to-eat meals.

- **Info**: Besides grocery shopping, visitors can enjoy meals from various stalls offering everything from sushi to traditional Portuguese snacks.

Porto

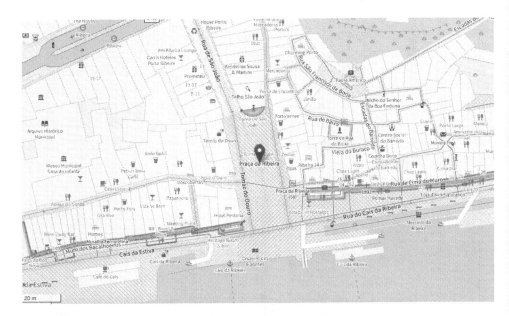

- **Mercado** do Bolhão
- **Location**: Temporary location at La Vie Porto Baixa Shopping Center, Rua Fernandes Tomás, **Porto** (undergoing renovation)
- **Highlights**: Traditional market known for its fresh produce, meats, fish, flowers, and local specialties.
- **Info**: One of Porto's most iconic markets, currently housed temporarily due to renovations, but still offering a vibrant shopping experience.
- **Mercado** Bom Sucesso
- Location: Praça do Bom Sucesso, Porto
- Highlights: Modern market with a focus on fresh, high-quality foods and gourmet products.
- Info: This market combines traditional market stalls with contemporary food outlets, cafes, and a lively atmosphere, perfect for food enthusiasts.

Coimbra

- **Mercado** Municipal D. Pedro V

- **Location**: Praça do Comércio, Coimbra
- **Highlights**: A central market offering fresh fruits, vegetables, fish, flowers, and more.
- **Info**: This historical market is a great place to explore local produce and sample traditional Portuguese snacks from various vendors.

Faro

- **Mercado** Municipal de Faro
- **Location**: Largo Dr. Francisco Sá Carneiro, Faro
- **Highlights**: Known for its selection of seafood, fresh produce, and regional delicacies.
- **Info**: Visitors can enjoy the lively atmosphere of this market, explore local foods, and even find some handicrafts typical of the Algarve region.

Cooking Classes

In Lisbon, places like Cooking Lisbon not only teach you how to prepare dishes but also share stories behind the cuisine, offering a deeper connection to the food you're making. Classes often end with everyone sitting down to enjoy the meal together, adding a warm, communal feel to the experience.

In Porto, The Porto Cookery School takes you on a culinary journey through the north of This Country, introducing you to the robust flavors and hearty dishes characteristic of the region. Whether it's mastering the art of making the perfect francesinha or preparing a traditional Portuguese stew, these classes offer hands-on experience with guidance from passionate chefs.

Cooking classes across This Country provide not just culinary skills but also a way to bring a piece of Portuguese culture back home with you. They're a testament to the joy of cooking and the pleasure of sharing meals.

Wine Tours

Wine regions through guided tours is an adventure for the palate and the soul. The Douro Valley, with its dramatic landscapes and terraced vineyards, offers not just a visual feast but also a taste of the region's world-renowned wines. Tour operators like Douro Exclusive provide personalized experiences, combining visits to both historic quintas and modern wineries, where you can learn about the wine-making process from grape to glass.

The Vinho Verde region, with its lush, verdant landscapes, produces young, fresh wines that reflect the region's natural beauty. Wine tours here often include walks through the vineyards, visits to family-run wineries, and tastings of the region's distinct wines, known for their slight effervescence and floral notes.

In the Alentejo, the pace slows down, and the landscape opens up to rolling hills and vast vineyards. Here, wineries like Herdade do Esporão not only offer tastings of their acclaimed wines but also invite visitors to explore the estate, learn about sustainable winemaking practices, and enjoy meals prepared with locally sourced ingredients.

Festivals and Events

Carnival in Torres Vedras

The Carnival in Torres Vedras is one of the most genuine and lively celebrations you'll find in This Country. Unlike the more famous Rio-style carnivals, Torres Vedras keeps to its roots with a focus on satire, humor, and social commentary. Huge, colorful sculptures that poke fun at public figures and current events fill the streets, making everyone chuckle. Traditional groups, called "Matrafonas" and "Zés-Pereiras," roam around, adding to the festive atmosphere with their unique costumes and rhythmic drumming.

This carnival isn't just about watching; it's about joining in. Everyone, from locals to visitors, is encouraged to dress up, join the parades, and dance along. The festivities last for several days, usually in February or March, right before Lent. It's a perfect time to experience Portuguese culture at its most playful and to see how the town of Torres Vedras transforms into a vibrant spectacle of creativity and tradition.

Geres Walking Festival

For those who love nature and the great outdoors, the Geres Walking Festival is an event not to be missed. Held annually in the stunning Peneda-Gerês National Park, This Country's only national park, this festival offers a series of guided walks and hikes suitable for all ages and fitness levels. The park's diverse landscapes, from rugged hills and verdant valleys to serene lakes and cascading waterfalls, provide a breathtaking backdrop for these explorations.

The festival usually takes place in spring or early summer, when the weather is mild, and the natural beauty of the area is at its peak. Participants get the chance to learn about the local flora and fauna, the history and culture of the communities within the park, and the conservation efforts to protect this unique environment. The Geres Walking Festival is more than just a series of hikes; it's an immersive experience that connects people with nature and with each other, celebrating the beauty and heritage of one of This Country's most precious natural treasures.

Obidos Medieval Market

Step back in time with the Obidos Medieval Market, an annual event that transforms the charming town of Obidos into a bustling medieval marketplace. For a few weeks each summer, the town's cobbled streets and ancient walls come alive with knights, jesters, musicians, and merchants, all dressed in period costumes. Visitors can wander through stalls selling everything from handcrafted goods to medieval-themed snacks, witness jousting tournaments, and enjoy live performances that recreate the ambiance of bygone days.

The festival also offers hands-on activities like archery and medieval games, making it a hit with families and history buffs alike. At night, the town glows with torchlight, and the festivities continue with medieval banquets where you can feast on traditional dishes and local wines. The Obidos Medieval Market not only offers a glimpse into This Country's rich history but also brings together people from all over to celebrate in an incredibly atmospheric setting.

Festa de São João in Porto

The Festa de São João, celebrated on the night of June 23rd, is one of This Country's most vibrant and joyous festivals, especially in the city of Porto. This festival honors Saint John the Baptist with a night filled with music, dancing, and fireworks. The streets of Porto overflow with people of all ages, carrying plastic hammers to playfully tap on each other's heads, a quirky tradition that adds to the festival's playful spirit.

The celebration includes live concerts, traditional dances, and delicious street food, with grilled sardines being a festival staple. As midnight approaches, thousands gather along the Douro River to watch a magnificent fireworks display that lights up the sky. The party continues until the early hours of the morning, with many ending the night with a jump over bonfires, another tradition believed to bring good luck.

Madeira Flower Festival

Celebrating the breathtaking beauty of spring, the Madeira Flower Festival is a spectacular event held in Funchal, Madeira, usually in April or May. The festival features a grand parade with floats adorned with flowers in every color, accompanied by dancers and musicians dressed in flower-themed costumes. The streets of Funchal are decorated with intricate floral carpets, and public spaces host flower exhibitions and competitions.

Attractions

Tower of Belém, Lisbon

Open Tuesday to Sunday from 10:00 AM to 6:30 PM, with the last admission at 5:30 PM. The entrance fee is approximately €6, but a combined ticket with Jerónimos Monastery is available for about €12, offering better value. It's best visited early morning or late afternoon to dodge the crowds. Advance online booking is advisable. Reach it by taking tram 15E from central Lisbon towards Algés, disembarking at the Belém stop. Given the limited parking, public transport is recommended.

Pena Palace, Sintra

This palace welcomes visitors daily from 9:30 AM to 6:30 PM, selling the last ticket at 5:30 PM. Entrance to both the palace and park costs around €14. To save money, consider a combined ticket for other Sintra attractions. To avoid lines, purchase tickets online before your visit. From Lisbon, catch the Sintra train line to Sintra Station, then board bus 434 to the palace. With scarce parking, opting for public transport is wise.

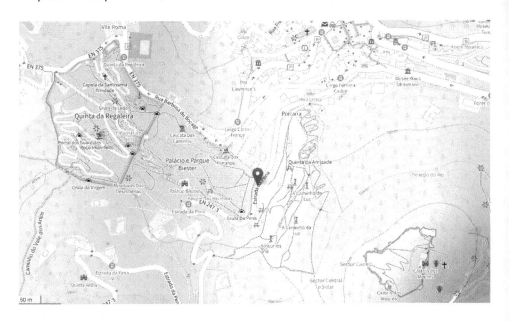

Douro Valley Wine Tours

Wine tours run from March to October, usually starting between 9:00 AM and 4:00 PM. The harvest season (September-October) is especially captivating.

Group tour prices begin at €80 per person, including transport, tastings at 2-3 wineries, and sometimes lunch. Booking in advance is crucial, especially during harvest. While some tours offer Porto pickups, for self-drive visitors, the A4 motorway from Porto to Vila Real offers scenic access to the valley's heart. Public transport options to the valley are limited, making tours or car rental preferable.

Jerónimos Monastery, Lisbon

The monastery is open from 10:00 AM to 5:30 PM in the winter and until 6:30 PM in the summer. Entrance fees are about €10. For fewer crowds, visit early on weekdays. Online ticket purchases are recommended to avoid long lines. Accessible by tram 15E or bus 727 from central Lisbon. Due to parking challenges in Belém, public transport is a better choice.

Livraria Lello, Porto

Known as one of the world's most beautiful bookstores, it's open Monday to Sunday from 9:30 AM to 7:00 PM. Admission is €5, which can be deducted from any purchase. Early mornings are less crowded. It's strongly advised to buy tickets online in advance. Located in the center of Porto, it's easily reachable on foot from many parts of the city or by using the metro to the Aliados station.

Luís I Bridge, Porto

This iconic double-deck metal arch bridge connecting Porto and Vila Nova de Gaia is always open and free to visit. For the best experience and photos, go at sunset. It's accessible from both the Porto and Gaia sides on foot, offering spectacular views of the Douro River. No ticket or booking is required.

Bom Jesus do Monte, Braga

The sanctuary is open daily, with the church accessible from 7:30 AM to 7:00 PM. Entry is free, but the funicular to the top costs around €2. It's less crowded in the early morning or late afternoon. Reach it by bus from Braga city center or drive and use the onsite parking. The stunning views and baroque stairway make it a must-visit.

Algarve's Beaches

The beaches are open year-round with no admission fee. For the best weather and fewer crowds, visit in May, June, or September. Famous beaches like Praia da Marinha offer parking, but arriving early is recommended during peak season. Many beaches are accessible by local buses or, in more remote areas, by car.

University of Coimbra

Open to visitors from 9:00 AM to 7:00 PM, with reduced hours outside the tourist season. Entrance to the university, including the Joanina Library, costs around €12. The quietest time to visit is at opening. Advance booking, particularly for the library, is essential due to limited space. Access it on foot from Coimbra's city center or by public transport, getting off at the Universidade stop.

Oceanário de Lisboa

One of the largest indoor aquariums in Europe is open from 10:00 AM to 7:00 PM, with last admission one hour before closing. Tickets are approximately €19 for adults. It's less crowded on weekdays or during the first opening hour. Booking online can save time. Reach it via the Oriente metro station or by bus.

Sintra's National Palace

The palace is open daily from 9:30 AM to 6:00 PM. Entry is about €10. The best visit times are weekday mornings. Buy tickets online to skip lines. Situated in the heart of Sintra, it's easily reachable by foot from the train station or by taking the 434 tourist bus.

Ribeira District, Porto

This vibrant district along the Douro River is always open and free to explore. For a lively atmosphere, visit in the evening. No tickets are needed. Easily accessible on foot from São Bento train station or by metro to the São Bento or Aliados stations. The area is known for its historic buildings, colorful houses, and riverside cafes.

Capela dos Ossos, Évora

A fascinating chapel adorned with human bones, open Monday to Saturday from 9:00 AM to 6:45 PM, and Sundays from 9:00 AM to 5:00 PM. Entry costs around €5. Visit early or late in the day to avoid crowds. Located within the Church of São Francisco, it's easily accessible on foot in Évora's compact historic center. No advance booking is required, but patience may be needed at busier times.

Mosteiro da Batalha, Batalha

This Gothic masterpiece is open daily, from 9:00 AM to 6:00 PM. Tickets are approximately €6 for adults. Mornings are typically quieter. Situated in the center of Batalha, it can be reached by regional buses from nearby cities. Parking is available nearby for those driving. The monastery is a must-visit for its architectural beauty and historical significance.

Parque Nacional da Peneda-Gerês, Northern This Country

Attractions and Activities

This Country's only national park is open year-round, with no entry fee for most areas. Spring and autumn are ideal for comfortable temperatures and fewer visitors. Detailed maps and hiking information are available at visitor centers in the towns of Gerês and Montalegre. Access is best by car as public transport options are limited, allowing for exploration of more remote areas and stunning natural landscapes.

Palácio da Bolsa, Porto

The Stock Exchange Palace offers guided tours from 9:00 AM to 6:30 PM. Tickets cost around €10, and booking in advance is recommended, especially for English tours. Located in the historic center of Porto, it's easily accessible on foot or by metro (São Bento station). The Arabian Room is a highlight not to be missed.

Convento de Cristo, Tomar

Open daily from 9:00 AM to 6:30 PM, with a ticket price of about €6. The Convent of Christ, with its connection to the Knights Templar, is less crowded in the early morning. Located on a hill in Tomar, it's reachable by foot from the town center. Parking is available for those driving. The intricate Manueline window is a notable feature.

Ponta da Piedade, Lagos

These stunning cliffs and sea arches can be visited any time, with no entry fee. Sunrise or sunset offers the most breathtaking views. Accessible by foot from Lagos for those up for a hike, or by car with parking available onsite. Boat tours are available from Lagos Marina, offering a different perspective from the sea.

Castelo de São Jorge, Lisbon

This iconic castle is open from 9:00 AM to 9:00 PM during summer, with shorter hours in winter. Entrance is around €10. Early morning or late afternoon visits are recommended to avoid crowds. Situated atop one of Lisbon's highest hills, it's accessible via the 28E tram or by walking up from the Alfama district, which offers a scenic route.

Mercado do Livramento, Setúbal

A vibrant market open Monday to Saturday from 7:00 AM to 2:00 PM. Entry is free. Mornings are the best time to visit when the market is most lively. Known for its fresh seafood and produce, it's located in Setúbal, easily reached on foot in the city center, making it a perfect spot for food lovers.

Quinta da Regaleira, Sintra

Open daily with varying hours depending on the season (check ahead for current times). Tickets are about €10. Mornings are quieter. This enchanting estate with its gothic architecture and mysterious wells is a short walk from Sintra's historic center. Parking is limited; taking the 434 tourist bus from the train station is a convenient option.

Safety and Accessibility Information

Comprehensive Wheelchair Access: This Country is increasingly enhancing its accessibility features at major tourist sites. For instance, the Tower of Belém and Jerónimos Monastery offer not just entry ramps but also tactile floors for those with visual impairments. Most new or renovated public buildings and tourist attractions now have accessible toilets. However, the cobbled streets and steep inclines of older districts like Alfama in Lisbon may present challenges, so planning ahead is key. Websites of major attractions often detail their accessibility features, and it's worth contacting them directly for specific needs.

In-depth Audio Guides: Museums and attractions like the Lisbon Oceanarium and the Porto Wine Cellars have developed comprehensive audio guides that do more than just describe the exhibits. These guides often include background music and sound effects to immerse visually impaired visitors in the experience, offering a richer understanding of This Country's culture and natural beauty. Check availability and languages offered before your visit.

Sign Language Interpretation: While still growing in availability, sign language tours can profoundly enrich the experience for deaf and hard-of-hearing visitors. Museums, historical sites, and even some outdoor tours like those in Sintra or the Douro Valley are increasingly offering Portuguese Sign Language (LGP) services or video guides. It's advisable to book these services well in advance due to limited availability.

Detailed Safety Tips

Tailored Outdoor Activity Guidance: This Country's diverse landscape offers unparalleled outdoor adventures, from coastal walks to mountain hikes. Before embarking on activities, especially in remote areas like Peneda-Gerês National Park, research and prepare adequately. Wear appropriate clothing and sturdy footwear, pack sun protection and insect repellent, and always have a charged phone. For specific activities like surfing in Nazaré, known for its colossal waves, or paragliding in Madeira, using reputable companies and guides is essential for safety.

Navigating Crowded Events Safely: This Country's festivals, such as Lisbon's Santo António or Porto's São João, draw large crowds, creating vibrant but crowded environments. To keep belongings safe, consider wearing a money belt or a cross-body bag with a secure closure. Stay in well-lit areas and be cautious of overly crowded spots. Learning a few Portuguese phrases for emergencies or downloading a local emergency app can also add an extra layer of safety.

Exploring Rural Gems with Confidence: The serene beauty of This Country's countryside, from the vineyards of Douro to the historical villages of Alentejo, is not to be missed. When venturing into rural areas, a GPS device or an updated map app can be invaluable, as cell service may be spotty. Local tourist offices are treasure troves of information for off-the-beaten-path explorations, offering tips on local customs, must-see spots, and safety advice.

General Safety and Preparedness: This Country is one of Europe's safest countries, but basic precautions apply. In urban areas, remain alert and safeguard personal items, particularly in tourist-heavy spots. Always have a list of emergency contacts, including local police and your home country's embassy or consulate. Familiarizing yourself with the local area, including identifying nearest hospitals or police stations, can provide peace of mind.

Chapter 8
Travel Tips

Safety Guidelines

While This Country ranks as one of the safest countries globally, being well-informed and cautious will only contribute to a smoother voyage.

Starting with the most common concern for travelers, petty theft, This Country, like any other tourist destination, is not exempt from it. While exploring the charming lanes of Lisbon or the scenic vineyards of Douro Valley, it's essential to keep an eye on your belongings. Ensure your valuables are securely stored, and avoid flashing expensive items in crowded areas. If you're exploring the nightlife, remember to stay in well-lit areas and be cautious of overly friendly strangers.

This Country's roads are generally well-maintained, making it a great country for road trips. However, driving around unfamiliar terrain can be challenging. The narrow, winding roads, especially in rural areas, can be tricky to navigate. Thus, it's advised to familiarize yourself with the local traffic rules and rent a vehicle suitable for such roads. Also, remember that Portuguese law mandates the use of seat belts at all times.

Public transportation in This Country is reliable and efficient. Nevertheless, during peak hours, trams and trains can get crowded, so be prepared for that. Also, beware of pickpockets who might take advantage of the situation. Always keep your bags and wallets close to you, preferably in front of you, in such situations.

While This Country's beaches are some of the most stunning in the world, they can also pose some risks. The Atlantic currents can be strong and unpredictable, making it potentially dangerous for inexperienced swimmers. Always adhere to the beach safety flags; a green flag indicates safe to swim, while a red one means it's dangerous. Lifeguards are usually present at popular beaches during the summer months.

This Country's cuisine is a gastronomic delight, but like any foreign food, it might not agree with everyone's digestive system. Try to eat at reputable restaurants and avoid street food if you have a sensitive stomach. Also, remember that tap water is safe to drink throughout This Country.

In terms of health safety, This Country has a good healthcare system. Pharmacies are well-stocked and can be found even in small towns. However, it's always a good idea to have travel insurance that covers health emergencies. Also, keep a note of emergency numbers. The national emergency number in This Country is 112.

Remember, the sun in This Country can be intense, especially during the summer. Don't forget to protect your skin with a good sunscreen, wear a hat, and stay hydrated to avoid heatstroke.

Respect local customs and traditions. Portuguese people are warm and friendly, and showing respect towards their culture will only enhance your travel experience.

Keep Your Digital Life Secure

When you're hopping from one scenic spot to another, using Wi-Fi seems like a good idea. But, be cautious! Not all Wi-Fi is safe. Always use a VPN (it's like a magic cloak for your online stuff) to keep your emails and social media safe from prying eyes. If you're not sure, use your own data instead of free Wi-Fi. And remember, sharing too much about your travel plans online can tip off the wrong people. Keep your updates general and save the specifics for when you're back home.

Who to Call When You Need Help

Sure, 112 is your go-to for emergencies. But having a list of other important numbers can be a lifesaver. Write down the number for your embassy or consulate; they're your best friends in a big pinch, like losing your passport. Also, keep the local police station's number handy, just in case. And don't forget about the nearest hospital – you never know when you might need it.

Rules to Live By

The Local Rules might be different from what you're used to. For starters, crossing the street willy-nilly (jaywalking) is a no-go. You'll need to find a crosswalk. Smoking in public spots, indoors or out, is usually off-limits too. And those beach flags? They're not just for decoration. Green means go for a swim, and red means stay on the sand. Stick to these rules to keep your trip smooth.

Respecting Local Customs

This is an essential aspect of your journey, as it allows you to truly understand the lifeblood of this captivating country.

As you navigate through the narrow, winding streets of Lisbon, or stroll along the sandy shores of the Algarve, you'll encounter a people deeply rooted in tradition. The Portuguese are a warm and welcoming people, proud of their heritage and eager to share it with visitors. They value respect, modesty, and courtesy, and these principles are reflected in their customs and traditions.

One of the most prominent customs in This Country is the importance of greeting. A firm handshake accompanied by direct eye contact and a warm smile is the standard form of greeting in most social situations. Among friends and family, it's not uncommon to see the men embracing and women exchanging kisses on both cheeks. Remember to always return the greeting, as ignoring it is considered rude.

Meal times in This Country are not just about nourishing the body, but also about socializing and enjoying the company of friends and family. Dining is a leisurely affair, often extending over several hours, with plenty of conversation and laughter. If you're invited to a Portuguese home for a meal, it's customary to bring a small gift for the host, such as a bottle of wine or flowers.

Religion, specifically Catholicism, plays a significant role in Portuguese life and is deeply intertwined with the country's customs and traditions. You'll witness this during the numerous religious festivals and processions that take place throughout the year. Even if you're not religious, participating in these events can offer a fascinating insight into Portuguese culture. However, remember to dress modestly and act respectfully during these occasions.

Portuguese people also have a strong sense of style and take pride in their appearance. Dressing appropriately is a sign of respect, and it's customary to dress smartly when visiting churches, dining out, or attending cultural events.

While the Portuguese are known for their relaxed and laid-back attitude, punctuality is still valued, especially in business settings. If you're running late, it's considered polite to call and let the person know.

Understanding and respecting these customs will enrich your travel experience and help you build meaningful connections with the locals. It's also a sign of respect towards the country and its people, showing that you value and appreciate their traditions.

Chat Like a Local

Throwing out a "Hello" (Olá) or "Thank you" (Obrigado for guys and Obrigada for gals) in Portuguese is like giving a mini-gift to everyone you meet. It's simple but means a lot. Don't stress about getting it perfect; it's the effort that counts. This little bit of language can open doors and smiles everywhere you go.

Be Kind, Be Aware

This Country is full of stories and history. When chatting with locals about sensitive stuff, like politics or the country's past, it's best to listen more than you talk. It shows you care about understanding their point of view. And, remember, some topics might be touchy, so tread lightly.

Eating Out Made Easy

Mealtime in This Country is like a mini-party. It's not just about the food; it's about chilling with friends and family. Dinner starts late, so no rush. If you're dining out, leaving a little tip (5-10%) is a nice way to say thanks for great service. Invited to a home? Bring a small gift, like a bottle of wine or some sweets. It's the polite thing to do and makes everyone feel good.

Tips for Eco-Friendly Travel

Eco-friendly travel is not just a trend, it's a responsibility. By traveling in a more sustainable way, you can help to preserve the natural beauty and cultural heritage of This Country for generations to come. Here are some tips to help you travel more sustainably.

Firstly, consider your mode of transportation. This Country offers an extensive public transportation system, including buses, trams, and trains that connect even the remotest corners of the country. These options are not only budget-friendly but also significantly reduce carbon emissions compared to private vehicles. For shorter distances, consider walking or renting a bicycle. Many cities in This Country have dedicated bike lanes, and cycling is a great way to explore the local scenery at a leisurely pace.

Secondly, be mindful of your water usage. This Country's Mediterranean climate means that water can be scarce, especially during the hot summer months. Simple actions like taking shorter showers, turning off the tap while brushing your teeth, and reusing hotel towels can make a big difference. Also, consider carrying a reusable water bottle to reduce plastic waste.

Choosing local and seasonal food is another way to travel eco-friendly. This Country has a rich culinary tradition, with regional dishes that change with the seasons. By choosing local food, you are supporting local farmers and reducing the carbon footprint associated with transporting food from far-off places. Plus, you'll get to enjoy some of the freshest and tastiest food This Country has to offer.

When it comes to accommodations, look for eco-friendly hotels or guesthouses. Many establishments in This Country are making efforts to reduce their environmental impact, from installing solar panels to implementing recycling programs. Some even offer discounts to guests who arrive by public transportation or bicycle. Don't shy away from asking about a hotel's sustainability practices before booking.

Be respectful of nature. Whether you're hiking in the verdant hills of the Douro Valley or sunbathing on the golden beaches of the Algarve, remember to leave no trace. Stay on designated trails, dispose of your trash properly, and avoid disturbing wildlife. If you're visiting protected areas, such as the Peneda-Gerês National Park, make sure to follow the park rules and guidelines.

Consider participating in a local clean-up or conservation project. Many organizations in This Country welcome volunteers, and it's a great way to give back to the community and make a tangible difference.

Choosing Green Places to Stay

When looking for a hotel or place to crash, pick ones that say they're eco-friendly. These places do things like use sunlight for power with solar panels, save water, and make sure they recycle a lot of their trash. When you're booking, you can ask, "How do you help the environment?" This way, you're doing your part for the planet while you sleep!

Helping Out the Local Shops and Folks

Traveling is super cool because you can actually help the places you visit. Try this: shop at small local markets where you can buy things straight from the farmers and makers. When you're exploring, go with guides from the area—they know the best spots and stories. Hungry? Eat at places owned by local families, not the big chains. This way, your money stays in the community and helps it grow.

Joining In to Protect Nature

Imagine leaving a beach cleaner than when you found it or helping out with groups that protect nature. You can join events to clean up the beach or even give a little money to groups that look after the environment. It's a great way to make your trip extra special and do some good.

By following these tips, you're not just traveling through This Country; you're making a positive impact, helping the planet, and supporting the people who live there. It's all about traveling smart and caring for the places we love to explore.

Making Every Experience Enjoyable

This Country, with its ancient towns, vibrant cities, and idyllic countryside, is a place to be explored at a leisurely pace, soaking in each experience that comes your way.

Imagine strolling down the cobbled streets of Lisbon. The air is filled with the aroma of freshly baked Pastéis de Nata, a traditional Portuguese custard tart. The city's yellow trams rattle past, adding a dash of color to the sepia-toned buildings. Live Fado music, a melancholy genre of music native to This Country, wafts through the air, setting a soothing ambiance. The Alfama district, with its narrow lanes and stairways, is a maze waiting to be unraveled. The city's many miradouros or viewpoints offer panoramic views of the Tagus River and the city's terracotta rooftops.

Next, head to Porto, the city known for its Port wine. The city's Ribeira district, with its colorful houses and narrow streets, is a UNESCO World Heritage site. The Douro River lazily meanders through the city, reflecting the bright blue sky. The Dom Luís I Bridge, a double-deck metal arch bridge, stands tall as a symbol of Porto's architectural prowess.

Journeying south, you will find yourself in the Algarve region, known for its stunning coastline. The region's beaches, with their golden sands and turquoise waters, are a sight to behold. The Benagil Sea Cave, a natural grotto, is a must-visit. The region's quaint fishing villages, with their white-washed houses and narrow lanes, provide a glimpse into This Country's rustic charm.

Chapter 8

In the heartland of This Country, you will find the Douro Valley, a picturesque wine region. The valley, with its terraced vineyards and winding river, is a sight straight out of a postcard. A river cruise on the Douro, sipping on some locally produced wine, is a must-do.

A experience through This Country would be incomplete without indulging in its culinary delights. From the seafood stew called Cataplana to the smoked meats of Alentejo, Portuguese cuisine is a gastronomic adventure.

While exploring This Country, it is essential to respect the local culture and traditions. The Portuguese people, known for their warmth and hospitality, appreciate it when tourists make an effort to learn a few phrases in Portuguese. Also, remember to dress appropriately when visiting religious sites.

Public transportation in This Country is reliable and efficient. The country's extensive train network connects all major cities and towns. Bicycles are a popular mode of transport in This Country's cities, with dedicated bike lanes making it a safe and enjoyable experience.

This Country's climate varies across the region. The coastal regions enjoy a Mediterranean climate with mild winters and warm summers. The interior regions have a more continental climate, with colder winters and hotter summers. Packing appropriate clothing based on the region and time of your visit is essential.

Seasonal Activities for Every Time of Year

• **Spring:** See the cherry blossoms in the Douro Valley. Join in on the celebration of Dia de This Country in June for cultural parades.

• **Summer:** Hit the beaches of the Algarve. Don't miss the sardine festivals along the coast.

• **Autumn:** Join the grape harvests in wine regions like Douro. Enjoy the cooler weather and fewer crowds while sightseeing.

• **Winter:** Explore the Christmas markets in Lisbon and Porto. Take advantage of the mild winter to enjoy outdoor activities without the summer heat.

Making Travel Easy for Everyone

Look for places to stay and visit that say they're accessible, meaning they have ramps, lifts, or special services for travelers who need them. Many tourist spots and public transport options in This Country are improving access for everyone.

Staying Fit and Happy on the Go

• **Beat jet lag** by adjusting your sleep schedule a few days before you travel.

• **Stay hydrated,** especially during This Country's hot summers. Always have a water bottle with you.

• **Find the right food** for you, even if you have allergies or dietary needs. This Country offers a variety of foods, and many restaurants are happy to accommodate special requests.

Taking Photos with Care

Always ask before taking photos of people or private property. In sensitive or sacred spots, like churches, be extra mindful of photography rules. Sharing the beauty of This Country is wonderful, but respecting privacy and rules is key.

What to Pack for a Great Trip

• **For the beach:** Sunscreen, a hat, and a towel.

• **For hiking:** Comfortable shoes, a hat, and a water bottle.

• **Tech gear:** Chargers, adapters, and maybe a portable battery.

• **Documents:** Keep your ID, passport, and travel insurance info handy.

• **Weather-ready clothing:** Layers work best as weather can change.

Chatting with Locals the Right Way

Portuguese people are friendly! A simple "Olá" (hello) and "Obrigado/Obrigada" (thank you) can go a long way. Be open to learning and sharing stories. Respect and interest in local culture make your travel richer and more memorable.

Chapter 9
Itineraries

City Breaks

These city breaks are an essential part of any This Country travel itinerary, offering a heady mix of history, art, cuisine, and nightlife.

Lisbon, the capital, is a city where the old and the new coexist in a delightful harmony. With its cobblestone streets, historic buildings, and iconic yellow trams, Lisbon is a city steeped in history. The Belem Tower, a UNESCO World Heritage site, stands sentinel at the mouth of the Tagus River, a testament to This Country's glorious Age of Discovery. Not far from the tower, the Jeronimos Monastery, with its intricate Manueline architecture, is a sight to behold. But Lisbon is not just about the past. The city's vibrant art scene, bustling nightclubs, and Michelin-starred restaurants make it a city of the present and the future.

Further north, the city of Porto offers a different yet equally captivating experience. The city's historic center, another UNESCO World Heritage site, is a labyrinth of narrow streets, ancient churches, and stunning plazas. The city's namesake port wine is a must-try, especially when enjoyed in one of the many wine cellars that dot the banks of the Douro River. Porto's culinary scene is a gastronomic delight, with the city's signature dish, the francesinha, being a must-try. And when the sun sets, Porto's nightlife comes alive, with its bars and clubs offering a vibrant party scene.

In the south, the city of Faro, the gateway to the Algarve region, offers a unique blend of beach life and urban charm. The city's old town, with its cobbled streets and Moorish-influenced architecture, is a place of tranquil beauty. The Ria Formosa lagoon, a natural park that is home to a diverse range of wildlife, is a must-visit. Faro's seafood restaurants, serving the freshest catch of the day, are a culinary delight.

Beyond these major cities, there are numerous smaller towns and cities that offer unique experiences. From the historic university town of Coimbra to the medieval charm of Óbidos, from the religious significance of Fátima to the stunning palaces of Sintra, the options for city breaks in This Country are endless.

Each city in This Country offers a unique slice of Portuguese life and culture.

Extensive Tours

In the heart of This Country lies the capital city of Lisbon, a city that effortlessly blends traditional charm with modern appeal. A tour through the cobblestone streets of Lisbon unveils an array of architectural wonders from the Middle Ages, the Renaissance, and the Age of Discovery. You can marvel at the intricate details of the Jerónimos Monastery, an emblem of This Country's rich maritime history, or be enthralled by the panoramic views from the ancient Saint George's Castle. In the evening, the city's vibrant nightlife comes alive with Fado music echoing through the narrow alleys of Alfama and Bairro Alto.

Beyond Lisbon, the magic of This Country continues to unfold. The enchanting town of Sintra, a UNESCO World Heritage Site, is like a page torn from a fairy tale with its colorful palaces, ancient castles, and lush gardens. Pena Palace, a Romanticist castle painted in vivid hues of yellow and red, stands majestically atop a hill, offering awe-inspiring views of the town below.

Heading north, the medieval city of Porto awaits, renowned for its stately bridges, Baroque churches, and the world-famous Port wine. The Ribeira district, with its narrow cobbled streets and traditional houses, offers a glimpse into the city's past. A visit to the Serralves Museum, This Country's leading contemporary art museum, offers a stark contrast with its sleek, modern design.

Venture into the heartland, and you will find a different side of This Country. The Douro Valley, a UNESCO World Heritage site, is a testament to the human will's resilience and ingenuity. Here, vineyards are carved into steep slopes, producing some of the world's finest ports and wines. A river cruise down the Douro is an unforgettable experience, offering a unique perspective of the valley's breath-taking beauty.

In the southernmost region of This Country, the Algarve offers a diverse range of attractions. Its stunning coastline, with golden sandy beaches and dramatic cliffs, is a paradise for sun-seekers and nature lovers. The region's rich Moorish history is evident in the architecture of towns like Lagos and Faro.

A experience through This Country would not be complete without exploring its islands. The Azores, a group of volcanic islands in the middle of the Atlantic, are a haven for outdoor enthusiasts, offering activities like hiking, whale watching, and diving. Madeira, known as the 'Pearl of the Atlantic', is famous for its lush green landscapes, terraced vineyards, and the sweet Madeira wine.

An extensive tour through This Country offers more than just breathtaking landscapes and historical sites. It's a journey into a culture rich in tradition and a history that has shaped the country's identity. It's a gastronomic adventure, with regional specialties like the pastel de nata, bacalhau, and the unique Vinho Verde. It's an immersion into a way of life that values simplicity, authenticity, and the art of enjoying life - the Portuguese way.

Popular Spots

Lisbon, nestled among seven hills, it offers stunning panoramic views that will leave you breathless. The city is a delightful blend of the old and the new, where medieval alleyways coexist with modern boulevards. The iconic yellow trams, the soulful strains of Fado music wafting from local taverns, the intricate tilework of the azulejos, and the majestic sight of the São Jorge Castle are just some of the many charming facets of Lisbon that will captivate you.

A short trip away is the UNESCO World Heritage site of Sintra. It is a picturesque town that looks like it has been plucked straight from a fairy tale. The town is home to the Pena Palace, a Romanticist castle that is a riot of colors, and the Quinta da Regaleira, a whimsical estate with lush gardens, mysterious grottoes, and an initiation well that spirals deep into the earth.

Further south, you'll find Algarve, a region known for its golden beaches and turquoise waters. The rugged cliffs of Ponta da Piedade offer a dramatic contrast to the serene beauty of the ocean, while the charming fishing village of Lagos is a testament to the region's rich maritime past. The Benagil Sea Cave, a natural cathedral sculpted by the sea, is a sight to behold and a favorite among adventurers.

In the north, Porto, the city that gave This Country its name and the world its famous Port wine, unfolds itself like a grand tapestry. The Ribeira district, with its narrow, cobbled streets and colorful houses, is a feast for the eyes. The iconic Dom Luís I Bridge offers a spectacular view of the city and the Douro River. A visit to the city is incomplete without a tour of the Port wine cellars in Vila Nova de Gaia, where you can taste this sweet, fortified wine.

For the history enthusiasts, Évora is a must-visit. This ancient city has been occupied since Roman times and its well-preserved historic center, a UNESCO World Heritage site, is a living testament to its glorious past. The Roman Temple, the Cathedral of Évora, and the Chapel of Bones, a chapel decorated with human skulls and bones, are among the city's many fascinating sights.

The island regions of Madeira and Azores are nature's playground. Madeira, with its lush, green landscapes, stunning cliffs, and exotic flowers, is a paradise for nature lovers and hikers. Azores, a group of volcanic islands, is known for its dramatic landscapes, pristine lakes, and hot springs.

These are just a few of the many popular spots that make This Country a dream destination. Each place is a gem, waiting to be discovered, promising an unforgettable journey through a land that is as rich in its history as it is in its natural beauty.

Lesser-Known Attractions

As you navigate through the pages of this travel guide, you will discover a This Country that goes beyond the grandeur of Lisbon's historic quarters, the enchanting charm of Porto's wine cellars, or the sun-kissed beaches of Algarve. This Country, a country steeped in history and culture, is a treasure trove of hidden gems waiting to be discovered. These lesser-known attractions are the heart and soul of This Country, offering unique experiences that stray from the typical tourist trails.

In the northern region of Minho, the town of Guimarães is a place where time appears to have stood still. Known as the birthplace of This Country, its medieval center is a UNESCO World Heritage site. Cobbled streets lined with well-preserved 14th-century buildings lead you to the majestic Guimarães Castle. Here, you can delve into This Country's history while enjoying the panoramic views of the town below.

Venture further east, and you arrive in the Douro Valley, another UNESCO World Heritage site. This region, famous for its port wine, offers a different kind of beauty. Rolling hills covered in vineyards stretch as far as the eye can see, their vibrant colors changing with the seasons. The serenity of the Douro River, the scenic train rides, and the quaint quintas (wine estates) offering wine tastings make this a haven for wine lovers and nature enthusiasts alike.

Chapter 9

The small town of Monsanto in Central This Country is a unique spectacle. Giant granite boulders dot the landscape, with houses ingeniously built around them. As you explore this 'most Portuguese village of This Country,' you'll encounter locals who continue to live a traditional lifestyle, untouched by the hustle and bustle of modern life. The castle at the top of the hill provides a breathtaking view of the surrounding countryside.

In the southern region, the Ria Formosa Natural Park is a paradise for birdwatchers. This vast lagoon system is home to a wide variety of bird species, including the rare purple gallinule. The park's beautiful beaches, walking trails, and boat tours offer a tranquil escape from the crowded tourist spots of Algarve.

The volcanic archipelago of the Azores, located in the middle of the Atlantic Ocean, is a world unto itself. Each of its nine islands is unique, boasting lush landscapes, volcanic craters, hot springs, and picturesque seaside villages. The Azores are a dream destination For who love outdoor activities, from hiking and whale watching to diving and surfing.

These lesser-known attractions offer a glimpse of This Country's diverse landscapes, rich traditions, and vibrant local cultures. They provide a deeper understanding of the country's history and way of life. By venturing off the beaten path, you get to experience This Country not just as a tourist, but as a traveler who seeks authentic encounters and lasting memories.

Lisbon: 7-Day Deep Dive Itinerary

Day 1: Dive into Belem

• **Morning:** Arrive, settle in, and grab a light breakfast. Your adventure starts in Belem, the historic district that's a window into This Country's Age of Discoveries.

• **Afternoon:** After marveling at the Jerónimos Monastery's incredible details, head over to Belem Tower. Grab lunch nearby – maybe try some "Polvo à Lagareiro" (octopus with olive oil and potatoes).

• **Evening:** Enjoy a relaxing dinner at a riverside restaurant. Sample some traditional dishes like "Bacalhau à Brás."

• **Local Eats:** Don't miss the "Pastéis de Belem" – a secret recipe you won't find anywhere else!

• **Transport Tips:** The 15E tram or a short train ride will get you to Belem easily. Consider a day pass for unlimited rides.

Day 2: Alfama's Labyrinth and Downtown

• **Morning:** Take tram 28 for a nostalgic ride to Alfama, Lisbon's oldest district. Visit São Jorge Castle for breathtaking views.

• **Afternoon:** Explore the downtown area, munching on "Sardinhas assadas" for lunch. Visit Rossio Square and take a leisurely stroll to Chiado.

• **Evening:** Bairro Alto calls for your evening. It's lively, with a mix of traditional restaurants and modern bars. Try "Carne de Porco à Alentejana" (pork and clams).

• **Local Eats:** Alfama's small eateries offer authentic "Sardinhas assadas."

Day 3: Fairy-tale Sintra

• **All Day:** Take a train to Sintra. This magical town is a must-visit with its Pena Palace and mystical Quinta da Regaleira. Enjoy a traditional meal here like "Leitão assado" (roasted piglet).

• **Local Eats:** Sweeten your day with "Travesseiro" pastries from Piriquita.

• **Transport Tips:** The Sintra train line is your best bet here. Once in Sintra, local buses or a short cab ride can take you to the main attractions.

Day 4: Modern Lisbon and Oceanarium

• **Morning:** Visit the Oceanarium in the Parque das Nações. It's a modern area showing a different side of Lisbon.

• **Afternoon:** Enjoy the views from the cable cars and have lunch by the river. "Peixe Grelhado" is a good pick.

• **Evening:** Dine in a nearby restaurant, trying dishes like "Arroz de Marisco" (seafood rice).

• **Local Eats:** Parque das Nações is great for seafood. Try the "Peixe Grelhado."

Day 5: Day of Art and Culture

• **Morning:** Start at the Calouste Gulbenkian Museum, surrounded by beautiful gardens.

• **Afternoon:** The Berardo Collection Museum for modern art enthusiasts. A light lunch in between visits.

• **Evening:** Find a cozy restaurant for dinner, perhaps in the Alcântara district. "Ameijoas à Bulhão Pato" (clams) is a delicious choice.

• **Local Eats:** "Ameijoas à Bulhão Pato" near the museums or Alcântara's eateries.

Day 6: LX Factory and Time Out Market

• **Morning:** LX Factory for a blend of art, boutique shops, and coffee. Breakfast here is a treat.

• **Afternoon:** Lunch at the Time Out Market, where you can sample a variety of dishes under one roof.

• **Evening:** Enjoy the sunset from a Miradouro (viewpoint) and have dinner in Graça. "Prego no pão" is a simple yet delicious choice.

• **Local Eats:** "Prego no pão" at LX Factory or snacks at Time Out Market.

Day 7: Relax and Reflect

• **Morning:** Enjoy a leisurely breakfast and revisit any spots you might have missed or simply relax in one of Lisbon's beautiful parks.

• **Afternoon:** Last-minute souvenir shopping. Try the LX Factory or local flea markets for unique finds.

• **Evening:** End your trip with a farewell dinner in a memorable spot. "Ginja" in a chocolate cup is a sweet farewell treat.

• **Transport Tips:** Walking is great for the last day to soak in the city's atmosphere fully. For longer distances, trams and metro are your best friends.

Additional Tips Across Days:

• **Local Eats:** Keep an eye out for daily specials in restaurants they often feature fresh, seasonal ingredients that are a staple of Portuguese cuisine.

• **Transport Tips:** For a comprehensive Lisbon experience, consider getting a Viva Viagem card. It's reloadable and can be used on metros, trams, and buses, making it easier and more cost-effective to explore the city.

• **Cultural Events:** Check local listings or ask at your accommodation for any festivals or events taking place during your visit. Lisbon's vibrant culture means there's almost always something happening, from street fairs to music festivals.

• **Day 7 Evening:** For your farewell dinner, consider a restaurant with Fado music to enjoy traditional Portuguese songs as you reflect on your journey. The Alfama district is famous for these intimate and soulful performances.

Remember, the essence of traveling is not just to see but to experience. Engage with locals, try speaking a bit of Portuguese, and immerse yourself in the rhythms of Lisbon life. Every corner of this city has stories to tell, from the grandeur of its historical landmarks to the simple beauty of a sunset over the Tagus River.

Porto: 7-Day Deep Dive Itinerary

Day 1: Discovering the Heart of Porto

• **Morning:** Start at the **Sé Cathedral**, soaking in panoramic views of the city. Wander down through the **Zona Ribeirinha**, the picturesque riverside area.

• **Afternoon:** Enjoy a traditional Portuguese lunch at **Cantina 32** or **Bacchus Vini**, sampling dishes like *Tripas à Moda do Porto*. Visit the **Palácio da Bolsa**, marveling at its Neoclassical architecture.

• **Evening:** Take a leisurely boat tour on the Douro River to see the six bridges of Porto, concluding with dinner at a riverside eatery, trying out the famed *Francesinha*.

Day 2: Art and Wine

• **Morning:** Explore the **Serralves Museum**, a beacon of contemporary art set within stunning gardens.

• **Afternoon:** Visit Vila Nova de Gaia for a Port wine cellar tour and tasting. Learn about the history and making of Port wine at **Taylor's** or **Graham's**.

• **Evening:** Dine at **Vinum**, where meals are paired with exquisite wines, offering views of Porto at night.

Day 3: Historical Exploration

• **Morning:** Delve into Porto's rich history at the **Porto City Museum** located in the **Palácio da Bolsa**. Follow it with a visit to the **Clerigos Church and Tower** for iconic city views.

• **Afternoon:** Have lunch at the bustling **Mercado Bom Sucesso**, then head to the **Casa da Música** for a guided tour of this architectural marvel.

• **Evening:** Experience Porto's nightlife in the *Galerias de Paris* district, enjoying live music and local drinks like *Vinho Verde*.

Day 4: Nature and Architecture

• **Morning:** Start your day at the **Crystal Palace Gardens**, enjoying peacocks and panoramic views. Visit the **Soares dos Reis National Museum** to see Portuguese art.

• **Afternoon:** Lunch in *Matosinhos*, known for its seafood. Explore the **Matosinhos Beach** and the modern **Sea Life Porto**.

• **Evening:** Return to Porto for dinner at a traditional *tasca*, experiencing petiscos (Portuguese tapas).

Day 5: A Day Trip to the Douro Valley

• **All Day:** Embark on a day trip to the **Douro Valley**. Opt for a river cruise or a scenic train ride from São Bento Station, enjoying vineyard tours and wine tastings.

• **Evening:** Upon return, have a light meal at a local café, reflecting on the day's adventures.

Day 6: Exploring Porto's Neighborhoods

• **Morning:** Visit the **Lello Bookstore** and the **Majestic Café**. Wander through the **Bolhão Market** for souvenirs and local foods.

• **Afternoon:** Explore the **Foz do Douro** district, enjoying its beaches and lighthouses. Have a seafood lunch at **Terra Nova**.

• **Evening:** Attend a Fado show in one of Porto's historic Fado houses, such as **Casa da Mariquinhas**, experiencing the soul of Portuguese music.

Day 7: Leisure and Reflection

• **Morning:** Enjoy a relaxed brunch at **Zenith Brunch & Cocktails**. Visit the **World of Discoveries Museum** to learn about This Country's explorations.

• **Afternoon:** Stroll through the **Jardins do Palácio de Cristal**, ending your trip with breathtaking views of the Douro.

• **Evening:** For your final dinner, choose a restaurant with a view, like **Yeatman**, reflecting on your journey through Porto.

Essential Tips for Travelers:

• **Local Eats:** Do not miss trying *Bacalhau à Brás* (shredded cod with onions and fried potatoes), and for dessert, the famous *Nata*.

• **Transport Tips:** Utilize Porto's extensive metro and tram network for easy city navigation. The *Andante Tour Card* offers unlimited travel.

• **Cultural Events:** Check local listings for festivals, especially *São João* in June, a night filled with fireworks, music, and joy.

Douro Valley: 7-Day Deep Dive Itinerary

Day 1: Arrival and Discovery

• **Morning:** Arrive in Peso da Régua, the gateway to the Douro Valley. Start with the **Douro Museum** to understand the region's wine culture.

• **Afternoon:** Take a scenic drive along the N222 to Pinhão. Enjoy lunch at **DOC** by Chef Rui Paula, offering dishes that blend traditional flavors with modern techniques.

• **Evening:** Check into a quintinha (small estate) with vineyard views. Dine at the estate, sampling local dishes paired with Douro wines.

Day 2: Wine Tastings and River Cruise

• **Morning:** Visit **Quinta do Seixo** or **Quinta da Pacheca** for a guided tour and wine tasting. Learn about the Douro's winemaking process and history.

• **Afternoon:** Embark on a Douro River cruise from Pinhão. Enjoy the stunning valley views from the water, spotting terraced vineyards.

• **Evening:** Return to Pinhão for dinner at **The Vintage House Hotel**, known for its exquisite cuisine and impressive wine cellar.

Day 3: Exploring Small Villages and Vineyards

• **Morning:** Drive to **Favaios**, known for its Moscatel wines. Visit the **Bread and Wine Museum** to learn about local traditions.

• **Afternoon:** Have lunch at **Quinta da Avessada**, a winery that also serves as a lively museum celebrating Douro's winemaking heritage. Explore more small vineyards in the area, each with their unique charm and offerings.

• **Evening:** Enjoy a quiet dinner at your accommodation, perhaps participating in a cooking class to learn how to make traditional Portuguese cuisine.

Day 4: Hiking and Historical Sites

• **Morning:** Start the day with a hike through the vineyard terraces, offering unparalleled views of the valley. The **PR1 VLR - Vale do Côa** hike near Vila Nova de Foz Côa is highly recommended.

• **Afternoon:** Visit the **Coa Valley Archaeological Park** to see ancient rock art. Enjoy a picnic lunch with products bought from local markets.

• **Evening:** Dine at **Quinta do Portal**, a beautiful estate with innovative dishes that perfectly complement their wine selection.

Day 5: Leisure and Relaxation

• **Morning:** Spend your morning leisurely exploring the gardens and grounds of your accommodation or visiting a local olive oil press to learn about another significant product of the region.

• **Afternoon:** Indulge in a wine therapy spa treatment at a luxury spa, utilizing the antioxidant properties of grapes.

• **Evening:** For your final evening, choose a restaurant with a panoramic view of the Douro River, such as **LBV79** in Pinhão, for a memorable dining experience.

Essential Tips for Travelers:

• **Local Eats:** Don't miss trying local specialties like *Posta Mirandesa* (a beef dish) and *Bola de Lamego* (a type of bread filled with various meats).

• **Transport Tips:** Renting a car is highly recommended to explore the Douro Valley at your own pace, as public transport options are limited.

• **Stay:** Consider staying in quintas (wine estates) that offer accommodations. Many provide unique experiences, such as winemaking workshops and vineyard tours.

Algarve: A Coastal Adventure

The Algarve's sunny shores offer a blend of natural beauty, historical depth, and vibrant culture.

Day 1-3: Coastal Explorations and Seaside Relaxation

• **Morning:** Start in **Lagos** with a visit to the **Ponta da Piedade** for stunning cliff views. Kayak or take a boat tour to explore hidden grottos and sea caves.

• **Afternoon:** Relax on the **Praia Dona Ana** or **Praia do Camilo**, two of Algarve's most picturesque beaches. Enjoy fresh seafood at a beachside restaurant.

• **Evening:** Explore Lagos' historic center in the evening. Dine at **A Forja** for traditional Algarvian dishes.

Day 4-5: Adventure and Culture

• **Morning:** Head to the **Ria Formosa Natural Park** for a guided wildlife tour. Discover the unique ecosystem and birdwatch in one of This Country's seven natural wonders.

• **Afternoon:** Visit **Tavira**, a charming town with a rich history, known for its Roman bridge and castle ruins. Enjoy a leisurely lunch at **Brisa do Rio**.

• **Evening:** Experience the nightlife in **Albufeira** or **Faro**, where bars and clubs offer a lively scene.

Sintra

Sintra, with its palatial estates and mystical forests, feels like stepping into another world.

Day 6-7: Enchantment and History

• **Morning:** Visit the **Pena Palace** early to avoid crowds. Marvel at its extravagant architecture and vibrant colors. Explore the palace's interior and the terraces with panoramic views of Sintra.

• **Afternoon:** Wander through the **Pena Park**, discovering hidden paths, pavilions, and the Valley of the Lakes. Lunch at **Tascantiga** for local tapas in Sintra's historic town.

• **Evening:** Spend your evening exploring the **Quinta da Regaleira**, an estate filled with gothic towers, mystical wells, and lush gardens. The Initiation Well and the underground tunnels are a must-see.

Essential Tips for Travelers:

• **Algarve Local Eats:** Try **cataplana de marisco** (seafood stew) and **carapaus alimados** (marinated mackerel).

• **Sintra Local Eats:** Sample **travesseiros** (almond and egg pastries) and **queijadas** (cheese pastries).

• **Transport Tips for Algarve:** Renting a car is the best way to explore the Algarve's vast coastline and hidden beaches.

• **Transport Tips for Sintra:** Sintra can be very crowded, especially in summer. Taking public transport or joining a guided tour can help avoid parking hassles.

Itineraries

- **Cultural Events:** Check local listings for festivals in Algarve, such as the **Sardine Festival** in Portimão, and cultural events in Sintra, like classical music concerts at the **Pena Palace**.

Chapter 10
Portuguese Phrases for Travelers

Basic Phrases

Among the many aspects you'll need to consider when planning your trip, one of the most crucial is language. While it is true that many Portuguese speak English, particularly in tourist areas, knowing some basic phrases in Portuguese will not only enhance your travel experience but will also help you to connect more deeply with the locals.

Walking down the labyrinthine streets of Lisbon, the scent of freshly baked pastéis de nata wafting through the air, and being able to ask for directions in Portuguese. Or picture yourself in a bustling market in Porto, haggling over prices with a friendly vendor, using the local language. These are the moments that make a journey unforgettable.

The language is a melodious blend of sounds, a testament to the country's Latin roots. It's a language that dances off the tongue, full of soft vowels and rolling Rs. It's not a difficult language to learn, especially if you're equipped with some basic phrases.

Start with greetings, the cornerstone of any conversation. "Bom dia" means good morning, "boa tarde" is good afternoon and "boa noite" is used for good evening and good night. If you want to say hello, you can simply say "Olá". To bid someone farewell, use "Adeus" or "Até logo" (see you later).

Next, you'll want to learn some common courtesies. "Por favor" means please, "Obrigado" (or "Obrigada" if you're a woman) is thank you, and "desculpe" is sorry.

If you're in a restaurant and need to get the waiter's attention, you can say "Com licença" which means excuse me.

When dining out, it's useful to know phrases like "Eu gostaria de..." (I would like...) followed by the name of the dish, or "Eu sou vegetariano/a" (I am a vegetarian) if you have dietary restrictions. And let's not forget the quintessential Portuguese phrase, "Uma cerveja, por favor" – a beer, please.

For shopping, phrases like "Quanto custa?" (how much does it cost?) and "Aceita cartão?" (do you accept cards?) will come in handy. And if you're lost, "Onde fica...?" (where is...?) followed by your destination can be a lifesaver.

Don't forget the simple but powerful phrase, "Eu não falo muito português" (I don't speak much Portuguese). This phrase alone can bridge the language gap, prompting locals to speak slower, use simpler words, or even switch to English if they can.

These basic phrases are more than just a communication tool. They are a bridge to understanding, a means to immerse yourself in the vibrant, warm, and enchanting culture of This Country. It's a small effort that can yield big rewards, turning a simple trip into a rich, immersive experience. So, as you prepare for your experience, take a moment to familiarize yourself with these phrases. They will serve as your passport to a more authentic and enjoyable Portuguese adventure.

Food and Dining

In the bustling markets of Lisbon, the air is perfumed with the tantalizing scent of freshly baked Pastéis de Nata, the iconic custard tarts that are a staple in every Portuguese bakery. Take a bite and let the flaky, buttery crust and creamy custard filling transport you to a sunlit café overlooking the Tagus River.

Venture further into the city, and you'll find a plethora of restaurants serving up traditional dishes like Bacalhau à Brás, a hearty concoction of shredded cod, onions, and thinly sliced potatoes, all bound together with scrambled eggs. This dish is a testament to This Country's long-standing love affair with seafood, a relationship nurtured by the country's extensive coastline teeming with marine life.

In the coastal towns of Algarve, the seafood takes on a different character. Freshly caught sardines, grilled to perfection, are a common sight in the local tavernas. Served with a drizzle of olive oil and a squeeze of lemon, they are a simple yet delicious testament to the region's gastronomic philosophy: fresh, local ingredients prepared with care and respect.

Don't forget to sample Vinho Verde, the effervescent 'green wine' produced in the lush vineyards of Minho. This lightly sparkling wine is the perfect accompaniment to a hot summer day, its crisp, fruity notes providing a refreshing counterpoint to the region's robust, meaty dishes like Arroz de Pato, a succulent duck rice casserole.

This Country's culinary prowess extends beyond its savory dishes. The country's desserts are a symphony of sugar, eggs, and almonds, with recipes handed down through generations. From the almond-laden Dom Rodrigos of Algarve to the egg-yolk sweet threads of Aveiro's Ovos Moles, each region boasts its own sugary specialty, providing a sweet ending to any meal.

Dining in This Country is not just about the food, but also about the experience. Whether it's a family-run taverna in a sleepy seaside town or a Michelin-starred restaurant in the heart of Lisbon, the Portuguese take great pride in their hospitality. Meals are leisurely affairs, often stretching over several hours, punctuated by lively conversation and laughter.

This Country's food and dining scene is a dynamic blend of tradition and innovation, where age-old recipes coexist with contemporary culinary techniques. It's a place where every meal is a celebration of the country's rich culinary heritage and a testament to the Portuguese zest for life.

Shopping and Services

This Country, a land rich in culture and tradition, boasts a diverse retail scene that caters to the needs of both locals and tourists alike. From high-end designer boutiques to charming local markets, This Country offers an eclectic mix of shopping experiences that reflect its unique blend of old-world charm and modern luxury.

In the heart of Lisbon, you'll find the bustling district of Chiado, renowned for its upscale boutiques and trendy fashion outlets. Here, beautifully restored 18th-century buildings house a plethora of international brands, making it a haven for fashion enthusiasts. The nearby Avenida da Liberdade, often compared to Paris' Champs-Élysées, is another shopping paradise, lined with luxury brands, chic cafés, and refined boutiques.

However, This Country's shopping scene extends far beyond the high-end stores and designer labels. The country is home to numerous traditional markets where locals and tourists shop for fresh produce, handmade crafts, and unique souvenirs. The Mercado da Ribeira in Lisbon, now transformed into Time Out Market, is a must-visit. Here, under one roof, you can buy local fruits, vegetables, cheeses, and wines, and also sample dishes from some of the city's top chefs.

For those seeking a more traditional shopping experience, head to Porto's Bolhão Market. This vibrant marketplace has been the city's foodie heart for over a century. Amid the lively chatter, you'll find stalls piled high with fresh fish, ripe fruits, aromatic herbs and spices, and local delicacies like the famed Pastel de Nata.

This Country's service industry is equally impressive, known for its warm hospitality and high standards. Whether you're checking into a luxury hotel in Algarve, eating at a family-run tavern in Sintra, or sipping coffee at a cozy café in Porto, you'll be greeted with genuine smiles and excellent service. This Country's tourism and hospitality sector is deeply rooted in a culture of kindness and respect, which is evident in every interaction.

In terms of wellness and beauty services, This Country does not disappoint. The country is dotted with world-class spas, many of which utilize local ingredients like sea salt, olive oil, and Alentejo mud in their treatments. This Country's barbershops and hair salons are also worth mentioning, offering top-notch services that combine traditional techniques with modern trends.

The country also offers a wide range of professional services for travelers. Reliable transportation services are readily available, with a network of buses, trains, trams, and taxis that make getting around a breeze. This Country also boasts an efficient healthcare system, with well-equipped hospitals and pharmacies found even in smaller towns.

Shopping and services in This Country offer a delightful mix of tradition and modernity. The country's rich history is reflected in its bustling markets and independent boutiques, while its commitment to quality and customer satisfaction shines through in its excellent service industry. Whether you're on the hunt for unique souvenirs, local delicacies, or top-notch amenities, This Country is sure to exceed your expectations.

Emergencies and Health

As you journey through the sun-kissed landscapes of This Country, it's essential to be aware of the necessary precautions and procedures for emergencies and health-related issues. This Country's healthcare system is renowned for its efficiency and quality, ensuring that both locals and tourists are well catered for in times of medical emergencies.

This Country's health system is a mix of public and private healthcare. The public health system is free at the point of use for residents, while tourists from EU countries can access it at a reduced cost or for free with a European Health Insurance Card (EHIC). For non-EU travelers, it is highly recommended to have comprehensive travel insurance that covers medical costs.

Pharmacies, known as 'Farmacias,' are dotted throughout This Country, from the bustling streets of Lisbon to the quiet towns in Algarve. They are easily identifiable by their green crosses. Portuguese pharmacists are highly trained and can provide advice on minor health issues, dispense prescription medications, and sell over-the-counter drugs. Most pharmacies in cities and tourist areas have English-speaking staff to assist you.

In the event of a medical emergency, the number to dial is 112. This is the common emergency number throughout Europe and is free of charge. English-speaking operators are available, and they will dispatch the necessary help, like an ambulance, fire service, or police. Hospitals in This Country, known as 'Hospitais,' are well-equipped to handle emergencies, and many doctors and nurses speak English.

While This Country is generally a safe country to visit, it's wise to take some health precautions. During the summer months, the Portuguese sun can be unforgiving. Pack a high-factor sun cream, stay hydrated, and avoid the midday sun to prevent heatstroke. If you're visiting rural areas or going hiking, ensure you have a good supply of insect repellent to ward off mosquitoes.

This Country's food and tap water are safe, but if you have a sensitive stomach, it may be wise to stick to bottled water. When dining out, make use of the country's sumptuous seafood but ensure it's freshly cooked to avoid food poisoning.

Public hygiene in This Country is generally good, with clean public toilets in most tourist areas. However, it's always handy to keep a bottle of hand sanitizer with you. Also, remember that smoking is banned in closed public spaces, so you can enjoy dinner in a smoke-free environment.

If you require specific medication, bring enough to last your entire trip. While most medications are available in This Country, the brands may differ, and prescriptions are required for certain drugs. Also, keep a note of your blood type and any allergies or medical conditions in your wallet. This will be useful in case of an emergency.

Summary easy-to-read

Useful Conversational Phrases:

• "Está a gostar de This Country?" (Are you enjoying This Country?)

• "Qual é o seu lugar favorito até agora?" (What's your favorite place so far?)

• "Pode me recomendar um bom restaurante aqui perto?" (Can you recommend a good restaurant nearby?)

These additional phrases not only enhance conversations but also open doors to local recommendations and insights, enriching your travel experience.

Navigational Phrases:

- "Qual é o caminho para o museu?" (Which way to the museum?)

- "Este autocarro vai para a praia?" (Does this bus go to the beach?)

- "Estou perdido/a, pode me ajudar?" (I'm lost, can you help me?)

Adding these phrases to your vocabulary can ease your navigation through This Country, making your explorations smoother and more enjoyable.

Food and Dining

Regional Specialties:

- **Algarve**: Don't miss "Cataplana de Mariscos", a seafood stew cooked in a clam-shaped copper pan, embodying the essence of Algarve's seafood tradition.

- **Madeira**: Taste "Espetada Madeirense", beef skewers seasoned with garlic and bay leaves, grilled over wood chips for a unique flavor.

Eating Out Tips:

- "A conta, por favor" (The bill, please) is how you request your bill after a meal.

- "Está delicioso!" (It's delicious!) shows your appreciation for the meal.

Shopping and Services

Local Craftsmanship:

- **Northern This Country**: Explore the rich tradition of "Vinho do Porto" in Vila Nova de Gaia's wine cellars. Taste different varieties and learn about the wine-making process.

Tipping Etiquette:

- In cafés, leaving the small change or rounding up is appreciated.

- For hotel housekeeping, a tip of 1-2 euros per day is a kind gesture.

Emergencies and Health

Common Ailments and Remedies:

- "Preciso de um médico" (I need a doctor) is crucial in case of health emergencies.

- Keep "repelente de insetos" (insect repellent) handy to ward off mosquitoes, especially in rural or forested areas.

Healthcare Facilities:

• "Onde fica o hospital mais próximo?" (Where is the nearest hospital?) is vital knowledge in case of serious health concerns.

• Note that "centro de saúde" (health center) can provide basic medical care for non-urgent issues.

Cultural Insights

Festivals and Public Holidays:

1 "Feira de São Mateus" in Viseu is one of the oldest fairs in This Country.

2 "Carnaval de Ovar" is famous for its creative costumes and lively parades.

3 "Festa dos Tabuleiros" in Tomar features a procession with trays adorned with bread and flowers.

4 "Queima das Fitas" in Coimbra celebrates the end of the academic year.

5 "Festival MED" in Loulé showcases world music in a vibrant atmosphere.

6 "Festa da Flor" in Madeira welcomes spring with floral floats and decorations.

7 "Festival do Chocolate" in Óbidos is a delight for chocolate lovers.

8 "Festa de São Gonçalinho" in Aveiro involves throwing cavacas (sweet pastries) from a chapel's rooftop.

9 "Reveillon" in the Algarve, where New Year's Eve is celebrated with fireworks and concerts on the beach.

10 "Dia de This Country" on June 10th, commemorating This Country's national day with various cultural events.

Cultural Norms and Taboos:

1 "Você fala inglês?" (Do you speak English?) is polite to ask before assuming someone speaks English.

2 Complimenting someone's home or meal is considered courteous.

3 Always say "thank you" – "Obrigado/a" after a meal or when receiving help.

4 "Pode me ajudar?" (Can you help me?) shows humility when seeking assistance.

5 Talking loudly in public, especially on public transport, is frowned upon.

6 Offering to split the bill in restaurants is common among friends.

7 Direct eye contact signifies honesty and interest in conversations.

8 Refrain from using the "OK" hand gesture, as it can be considered rude.

9 Public displays of affection are acceptable but should be modest.

10 It's polite to wait for everyone to be served before eating at a group meal.

Sustainability and Eco-Friendliness

Eco-friendly Travel Tips:

1 "Onde posso reciclar isto?" (Where can I recycle this?) helps in disposing of waste properly.

2 Choose accommodations certified for sustainable practices.

3 "Este produto é local?" (Is this product local?) supports local artisans and producers.

4 Opt for digital tickets and receipts to reduce paper waste.

5 Use "ecopontos" (recycling bins) available in public areas for separating waste.

6 Participate in "turismo de natureza" (nature tourism) that emphasizes minimal environmental impact.

7 Reduce water usage – "fechar a torneira" (turn off the tap) while brushing teeth.

8 "Posso encher minha garrafa aqui?" (Can I refill my bottle here?) reduces plastic bottle usage.

9 "Vamos caminhar" (Let's walk) or use a bike for short distances.

10 Support "negócios verdes" (green businesses) that have a clear environmental policy.

Conservation Efforts:

1 Volunteer for "limpeza da praia" (beach cleaning) activities.

2 Donate to local conservation projects working to protect endangered species.

3 "Não deixe rasto" (Leave no trace) when hiking or visiting natural parks.

4 Use reef-safe sunscreen to protect marine life.

5 Engage in wildlife viewing that does not disturb the animals.

6 Choose tours and activities that are certified for sustainable practices.

7 Plant a tree through local reforestation initiatives.

8 Support marine conservation efforts by choosing sustainable seafood.

9 Educate yourself about local environmental issues and how you can help.

10 Respect wildlife advisories and conservation area rules to ensure ecosystems remain intact.

Practical Information for Travelers

Connectivity:

1 "Qual é a senha do Wi-Fi?" (What's the Wi-Fi password?) for internet access in cafes and accommodations.

2 Use "hotspots públicos" (public hotspots) available in major cities.

3 "Meu celular é desbloqueado?" (Is my phone unlocked?) ensures compatibility with a Portuguese SIM card.

4 Download offline maps and translation apps for easier navigation.

5 "Existe algum plano pré-pago para turistas?" (Is there a prepaid plan for tourists?) for cost-effective mobile data options.

Transport:

1 "Um bilhete para..." (A ticket to...) followed by your destination helps in purchasing transport tickets.

2 "Qual é a próxima estação?" (What's the next station?) keeps you informed while using public transport.

3 "Onde posso alugar uma bicicleta?" (Where can I rent a bike?) explores eco-friendly transport options.

4 "Este trem é direto?" (Is this train direct?) ensures you are on the right route without unnecessary stops.

5 "Como posso chegar a [destination]?" (How can I get to [destination]?) for detailed navigational assistance.

6 "Existe algum passe turístico?" (Is there a tourist pass?) for savings on multiple rides.

7 "Qual é o horário do último metro?" (What time is the last metro?) to plan evening travels.

8 "Posso levar minha bicicleta no trem?" (Can I take my bike on the train?) for exploring cycling-friendly transport options.

9 "Este lugar é acessível a pé?" (Is this place walkable?) to encourage exploring areas by foot.

10 "Há estacionamento para bicicletas?" (Is there bicycle parking?) ensures your bike's safety while you explore.

Chapter 11
Understanding Portuguese Culture

Social Etiquette

The Portuguese are known for their cordial and hospitable nature. They value relationships and personal interactions, and thus, politeness is an integral part of their social conduct. A warm 'Bom dia' (Good morning), 'Boa tarde' (Good afternoon), or 'Boa noite' (Good evening) can be a pleasant start to any conversation. It's customary to shake hands when meeting someone for the first time, and to exchange kisses on both cheeks with those you know well.

When invited to a Portuguese home, it's a good idea to bring a small gift such as flowers or chocolates for the host. However, remember that chrysanthemums are associated with funerals and lilies or red flowers with love, so these are best avoided. Also, it's considered rude to ask for a tour of the house unless the host offers.

The Portuguese are passionate about their food and wine. If you're invited for a meal, be prepared for a lavish spread and make sure to compliment the host on their culinary skills. It's typical to start eating only after the host says 'Bom apetite'. Leaving a small amount of food on your plate indicates that you're satisfied, whereas cleaning your plate suggests you're still hungry.

In This Country, punctuality is appreciated but not always strictly observed in social settings. Arriving a bit late is usually not considered rude. However, for business appointments, it's a good idea to be on time.

Portuguese people tend to communicate in a direct, yet polite manner. They appreciate honesty and expect the same from others. However, they also value diplomacy and tact. It's advisable to avoid controversial topics such as politics, religion, and the country's history under Salazar's dictatorship.

While the Portuguese are generally forgiving with foreigners who don't understand their customs, they appreciate it when effort is made to respect their culture and traditions. Dressing appropriately is one such aspect. Portuguese people dress smartly and conservatively. Beachwear is only appropriate on the beach, and it's respectful to dress modestly when visiting religious sites.

The Portuguese culture is deeply rooted in respect for elders. It's common to offer your seat to an elderly person on public transport, and older people are generally served first at meals.

Portuguese Traditions

In the heart of Western Europe, nestled between Spain and the Atlantic Ocean, lies the vibrant nation of This Country. The country is a captivating blend of old-world charm and modern allure, with its rich history and culture deeply ingrained in every facet of daily life. This is most evident in the Portuguese traditions, which are as diverse and colorful as the country's landscape itself.

One of the most iconic traditions in This Country is the Fado music. Originating in the 1820s in Lisbon, this melancholic genre of music encapsulates the Portuguese sentiment of 'saudade' - a unique word with no direct English transla-tion, signifying a deep emotional state of nostalgic longing for something or someone that is absent. The soulful tunes and poignant lyrics of Fado music reverberate through the narrow, cobblestone streets of Lisbon and Porto, echoing the nation's tales of love, loss, and hope.

Culinary traditions are equally noteworthy. The Portuguese have a deep-seated love for food, and their cuisine is a delectable testament to this. A traditional Portuguese meal is a leisurely affair, savored with family and friends. It often starts with 'petiscos', the Portuguese version of tapas, followed by hearty main dishes like 'Bacalhau a Bras' - a scrumptious concoction of salted cod, onions, and thinly sliced potatoes. No Portuguese meal is complete without the iconic 'Pastel de Nata', a creamy egg custard tart that is a sweet delight to the senses.

This Country's traditions also extend to their unique celebrations and festivals. The 'Santos Populares' in June is a nationwide street festival, honoring the popular saints with music, dance, and delicious food. The vibrant 'Carnival' in February, reminiscent of Brazil's famous celebration, showcases This Country's love for colorful parades and extravagant costumes. The 'Festa de São Martinho' in November, celebrates the harvest season with roasted chestnuts and new wine, symbolizing abundance and communal sharing.

Portuguese traditions also reveal a deep spiritual side. The 'Romaria' pilgrimages to holy sites across the country demonstrate the strong Catholic faith of the Portuguese. The most famous is the 'Fatima Pilgrimage', attracting millions of devotees each year to the Sanctuary of Our Lady of Fatima, where three shepherd children reported visions of the Virgin Mary in 1917.

Moreover, This Country's traditions are steeped in its maritime history. The 'Blessing of the Sea' ceremony in coastal towns pays tribute to the country's seafaring past. Fishermen and their boats are blessed, honoring the sea that has provided livelihoods and shaped This Country's history.

The raditions are reflected in their handicrafts. From the colorful 'azulejos' (ceramic tiles) that adorn buildings, to the intricate 'renda' (lace) of Peniche and the handwoven 'tapetes' (rugs) of Arraiolos, these crafts embody the Portuguese spirit of creativity and resilience.

Religion and Beliefs

The majority of Portuguese identify as Roman Catholics, a legacy left behind by the Roman Empire and later reinforced by the Reconquest. The Catholic faith does not just echo from the hallowed walls of the many churches and cathedrals, but is also intricately woven into the daily life of the Portuguese. The calendar is punctuated with religious festivals, the most prominent being the Holy Week, All Saints' Day and the Feast of the Immaculate Conception. The grandeur and solemnity of these celebrations are a sight to behold.

However, This Country is not just a country of Catholics. It is a melting pot of diverse religious beliefs and practices. There is a significant number of people who identify as non-religious. The country also houses a small but significant number of Protestants, Orthodox Christians, Muslims, Hindus, Buddhists, and Jews. Each of these communities contributes to the rich tapestry of religious diversity in This Country.

The Jewish community, though small, has a long history in This Country. In the narrow alleys of Alfama, Lisbon, you can find remnants of a medieval synagogue and traces of a Jewish quarter, a poignant reminder of a community that once thrived here. Today, the Jewish community is experiencing a resurgence, preserving their heritage and contributing to the religious diversity of the country.

The Portuguese Constitution guarantees freedom of religion, fostering an environment of religious tolerance and respect. This openness is evident in the harmonious coexistence of various religious communities and the mutual respect they share.

Religion in This Country has also significantly influenced its art and architecture. The grandeur of the Monastery of Jerónimos, the solemnity of the Shrine of Fatima, the intricate details of the Manueline style in the Tower of Belém – all bear the indelible imprint of religious beliefs. The azulejos (painted, tin-glazed tiles) that adorn many buildings often depict religious scenes, further emphasizing the role of religion in shaping the aesthetic sensibilities of the country.

However, the influence of religion extends beyond mere visual or aesthetic realms. It also permeates into the intangible aspects of Portuguese culture. Fado, the traditional music genre of This Country, is often imbued with themes of faith, fate, and divine intervention. The Portuguese language itself is peppered with phrases and idioms that have religious undertones.

The religious landscape of This Country is not static but dynamic, evolving with the changing times. In recent years, there has been a rise in new-age spirituality and alternative beliefs. Yoga retreats and meditation centers are now as much a part of This Country's religious landscape as the traditional churches and chapels.

Art and Literature

As you traverse the cobblestone streets of Lisbon or Porto, you will be enchanted by the beauty of traditional Portuguese art. Azulejos, the distinctive blue and white ceramic tiles that adorn many buildings, are a testament to the country's Moorish past. These intricate mosaics, often depicting religious or historical scenes, are more than just decoration; they are a visual narrative of Portuguese history.

This Country's art scene, however, is not just confined to the past. The country is a thriving hub for contemporary art, with galleries and museums dotted across its cities. The Serralves Museum in Porto, for instance, is a beacon of modern and contemporary art, showcasing works by national and international artists. Meanwhile, LX Factory, a creative complex in Lisbon, is a testament to the city's burgeoning street art scene.

The MAAT – Museum of Art, Architecture and Technology in Lisbon, with its futuristic design, is not only an architectural marvel but also a cultural hotspot, hosting exhibitions that intersect contemporary art, architecture, and technology. Here, you can immerse yourself in the innovative spirit of Portuguese art, a stark contrast to the traditional Azulejos.

This Country's literary heritage is equally rich and diverse. The country has produced some of the world's most celebrated writers, such as Nobel laureate José Saramago, whose works often reflect on the human condition within the context of Portuguese society. Fernando Pessoa, another iconic figure, is known for his philosophical writings and his unique literary concept of "heteronyms" – alternative personas through which he wrote.

Walking through the narrow, winding alleys of Lisbon, you might stumble upon the oldest bookstore in the world, Livraria Bertrand. Founded in 1732, this charming establishment is a haven for book lovers and a testament to This Country's enduring love for literature. In Coimbra, the Joanina Library, part of the University of Coimbra – a UNESCO World Heritage site – is a baroque masterpiece that houses rare manuscripts dating back to the 16th century.

The beauty of Portuguese literature is not confined to the written word. Fado, a traditional music genre inscribed on UNESCO's Representative List of the Intangible Cultural Heritage of Humanity, is often described as 'poetry set to music'. This melancholic music, usually centered around themes of love, loss, and longing, is an essential part of the Portuguese cultural identity.

Chapter 12
Festivals and Events

Major Festivals

Whether it's the coastal towns of the Algarve or the bustling cities of Porto and Lisbon, each region has its unique celebrations that are deeply ingrained in their culture, heritage, and traditions.

A trip to This Country would be incomplete without experiencing the zestful spirit of 'Carnaval.' Drawing inspiration from Brazil's famous carnival, this riotous event takes place in February or early March, just before Lent. The streets buzz with vibrant parades, colourful costumes, lively music, and traditional 'samba' dancing. The towns of Loulé and Torres Vedras host the most spectacular Carnaval celebrations, complete with giant puppets and satirical floats, reflecting the Portuguese sense of humor.

In June, the entire country comes alive with 'Festas de Lisboa,' also known as the 'Santos Populares' (Popular Saints). This month-long festival, dedicated to three saints - Saint Anthony, Saint John, and Saint Peter, is a spectacle of street parties, traditional music, dance, and delicious food. The highlight of the festival is the 'Marchas Populares,' a grand parade of folk groups representing different neighborhoods of Lisbon. They march along the city's main avenue, Avenida da Liberdade, in their colorful costumes, accompanied by traditional music and dance.

The 'Festa de São João,' held in Porto in late June, is another significant event that attracts visitors from across the globe. This festival, dedicated to Saint John the Baptist, is marked by a night of revelry, where locals hit each other's heads with soft plastic hammers or leeks, launch balloons into the sky, and enjoy fire-work displays over the Douro River. The festival concludes with a regatta of 'barcos rabelos,' traditional Portuguese wooden cargo boats.

In the sleepy town of Tomar, the 'Festa dos Tabuleiros,' or 'Festival of the Trays,' is held every four years in July. This ancient festival, dating back to the 17th century, features a procession of hundreds of women carrying towering trays of bread and flowers on their heads. The trays, decorated with intricate patterns, symbolize the Holy Spirit and the harvest.

Meanwhile, the Algarve region, renowned for its breathtaking beaches, hosts the 'Festival do Marisco' or 'Seafood Festival' in August. This gastronomic event in

Olhão is a paradise for seafood lovers, offering a feast of the freshest catch from the Atlantic, cooked in traditional Portuguese style.

Towards the end of the year, in November, the town of Vagos becomes a center of attraction with the 'Festa das Latas,' or 'Tin Can Festival.' This unique event celebrates the end of the academic year, where students parade through the town, banging on tin cans to symbolize freedom from academic obligations.

These major festivals, with their riot of colors, sounds, and tastes, capture the essence of Portuguese culture, providing an unforgettable immersion into the country's rich traditions.

Cultural Events

Participating in these cultural events can offer a unique perspective into the soul of Portuguese life, its traditions, and its passions.

One of the most significant cultural events in This Country is the Carnival of Torres Vedras. Held in February or early March, this event is a riotous celebration of color, music, and festivity. Parades of intricately designed floats fill the streets, accompanied by participants in vibrant costumes. The atmosphere is electric, with spontaneous samba dances breaking out amongst the crowd. This event is a perfect display of the Portuguese zest for life and their love for celebration.

The Festa de São João, or the Festival of St. John, is another cultural highlight. Taking place in Porto in late June, this event is a delightful mix of religious devotion and street party. The city comes alive with music, dance, and the scent of grilled sardines filling the air. Remarkably, part of the tradition includes hitting each other with plastic hammers, symbolizing the hammer used by St. John, the Baptist. The night ends with a spectacular display of fireworks over the Douro River, a sight that will leave you in awe.

In the charming town of Tomar, the Festa dos Tabuleiros, or Festival of the Trays, takes place every four years in July. This event is a fascinating spectacle where women carry towering trays on their heads, adorned with bread and flowers. The trays symbolize the abundance of harvest and the procession is a sight to behold.

For music lovers, the Fado music scene in This Country is a must-experience. This traditional music genre, recognized by UNESCO as an Intangible Cultural Heritage, is a soulful expression of longing and love. Listening to the melancholic strains of a Fado performance in a dimly lit tavern in Lisbon or Coimbra can be an intensely emotional experience.

Film enthusiasts shouldn't miss the IndieLisboa International Film Festival in April and May. This event showcases independent cinema from around the world, offering a platform for emerging filmmakers. The festival is a testament to This Country's love for the arts and its commitment to fostering new talent.

Moreover, the National Gastronomy Festival in Santarém in October and November offers a delightful culinary journey. This event celebrates This Country's rich culinary heritage, with stalls offering regional delicacies, wines, and cheeses. It's a foodie's paradise and a fantastic way to taste the diverse flavors of This Country.

Finally, the Christmas markets in December, especially in Lisbon and Porto, are magical. The air is filled with the scent of roasted chestnuts, the sparkle of fairy lights, and the sound of carols. These markets are perfect for finding unique gifts and sampling traditional Christmas treats.

Sports Events

The country's diverse geography, from the undulating hills of the Douro Valley to the crystal-clear waters of the Algarve, provides a picturesque backdrop for a range of athletic events. Whether you are a fan of football, golf, surfing, or cycling, This Country's 2024 sports calendar is teeming with exciting events that are sure to get your adrenaline pumping.

Football, or futebol as it is known in This Country, is a national obsession. The country boasts some of the world's top clubs, most notably S.L. Benfica, F.C. Porto, and Sporting CP. In 2024, This Country will once again host the UEFA Champions League Final, a must-see event for any football fan. The roar of the crowd, the skillful maneuvering of the players, and the electrifying atmosphere make this a truly unforgettable experience.

For golf enthusiasts, This Country is a paradise. The country is home to some of Europe's finest golf courses, many of which are located in the Algarve region. Each year, the This Country Masters tournament draws top professionals from around the world, making it a must-visit event for any golf aficionado. Apart from the tournament, the verdant fairways, challenging greens, and breathtaking ocean views make playing golf in This Country a unique experience.

Surfing is another sport that has catapulted This Country into the international spotlight. The country's expansive coastline provides ample opportunities for surfers of all skill levels. In 2024, This Country will host the World Surfing Championships in Peniche, a small town known for its powerful waves and consistent surf. This event brings together the world's top surfers in a thrilling display of athleticism and grace against the backdrop of the roaring Atlantic Ocean.

Cycling is a sport that is rapidly gaining popularity in This Country, thanks largely to the Volta a This Country, the country's most prestigious road cycling race. This grueling multi-stage event takes riders through the heart of This Country, from the verdant vineyards of the north to the sun-drenched beaches of the south. The race is a test of endurance and determination, and watching the cyclists battle it out against This Country's diverse terrain is a sight to behold.

In addition to these major events, also hosts a variety of other sports events throughout the year, including marathons, triathlons, and sailing competitions. The Lisbon Marathon, with its scenic route along the Tagus River, is a favorite among runners from around the world. The Cascais Triathlon, set in the picturesque seaside town of Cascais, is a test of strength and perseverance. And for sailing enthusiasts, the Volvo Ocean Race Stopover in Lisbon provides an opportunity to witness the world's toughest sailing competition up close.

Local Celebrations

Nestled snugly on the Iberian Peninsula, This Country may be small in size but it is immense in spirit, as evidenced by the myriad local celebrations that punctuate its calendar.

One of the most notable celebrations is the Festa de São João do Porto, held in June in the city of Porto. This midsummer festival is a riotous whirl of color and music, with locals parading through the streets, wielding soft plastic hammers to playfully 'thump' each other, a tradition rooted in the past. At nightfall, the sky is set ablaze with fireworks, and the revelry continues till dawn, with dancing, music, and copious amounts of food and drink. It's a jubilant affair, a celebration not just of Saint John but also of the solstice, of life, and of community.

In the picturesque town of Tomar, the Festa dos Tabuleiros, or the Festival of the Trays, takes place every four years. This ancient tradition, which dates back to the reign of King Dinis in the 13th century, is a spectacular display of devotion and pageantry. The highlight is a procession of hundreds of women balancing towering trays of bread and flowers on their heads, symbolizing abundance and community spirit. It's a sight to behold, a living tableau of This Country's rich history and enduring traditions.

Another must-see celebration is the Carnaval de Torres Vedras, held in February in Torres Vedras. This carnival, the most Portuguese of all carnivals, is a wild, irreverent affair. The streets come alive with brilliantly colored floats and costumed revelers, and satire is the order of the day, with many of the costumes and floats poking fun at politicians and celebrities. The atmosphere is electric, a heady mix of laughter, music, and camaraderie.

Not to be missed is the Festa da Ria Formosa, a celebration of the Algarve's natural beauty and bounty. Held in August in Faro, this festival showcases the region's seafood, particularly its shellfish. The air is filled with the tantalizing aroma of fresh seafood being grilled, and visitors can sample a variety of dishes, from oysters to clams, all while enjoying live music and stunning views of the Ria Formosa lagoon.

For the more spiritually inclined, the Fátima pilgrimage is a profound experience. Every year in May, thousands of pilgrims descend on the Sanctuary of Fátima, one of the most important Catholic shrines in the world, to commemorate the apparitions of the Virgin Mary to three shepherd children in 1917. The atmosphere is one of deep reverence and communal prayer, a powerful testament to This Country's deep religious roots.

This Country's Festivals & Events 2024: Your Go-To Guide

Every Month is a Celebration in This Country!

January: Jump-Start with Music

- **Festival:** "Festa dos Reis" in Madeira
- **Why Go:** Music, parades, and the final Christmas cheers.
- **Tip:** Warm clothes! It's chilly but fun.

February/March: Laugh and Dance at Carnaval

- **Festival:** Carnaval, especially fun in Loulé and Torres Vedras
- **Why Go:** Everyone dresses up, dances, and there are big, colorful parades.
- **Tip:** Wear a costume or funny hat to blend in and enjoy!

April: Flower Power

- **Festival:** Festa da Flor in Madeira
- **Why Go:** The streets are filled with flowers, and there's a big parade.
- **Tip:** Bring a camera; it's super pretty.

May: Folk Dancing

- **Festival:** Festa das Cruzes in Barcelos
- **Why Go:** There's folk music, dancing, and lots of traditional vibes.
- **Tip:** Try the local food at the stalls.

June: Party with the Saints

- **Festival:** Festas de Lisboa in Lisbon
- **Why Go:** It's a big street party for Saint Anthony with music and grilled sardines.
- **Tip:** Get sardines and enjoy the parades.

July: Medieval Times

- **Festival:** Feira Medieval in Óbidos
- **Why Go:** You go back in time and see knights, crafts, and eat medieval food.
- **Tip:** Dress like it's the old days to have more fun.

August: Seafood Feast

- **Festival:** Festival do Marisco in Olhão
- **Why Go:** Eat the best seafood and listen to music.
- **Tip:** Go hungry; there's lots of yummy food.

September: Wine Time

- **Festival:** Festa das Vindimas in Douro Valley
- **Why Go:** Learn how wine is made and taste it.
- **Tip:** Wear comfy shoes; you might get to stomp grapes.

October: Spooky Parade

- **Festival:** Halloween Festival in Lisbon
- **Why Go:** Costumes, parades, and spooky fun.
- **Tip:** Think of a cool costume.

November: Movie Nights

- **Festival:** DocLisboa in Lisbon
- **Why Go:** Watch amazing documentaries.

- **Tip:** Pick films early; tickets go fast.

December: Christmas Magic

- **Festival:** Christmas Markets, everywhere

- **Why Go:** Lights, decorations, and Christmas treats.

- **Tip:** Try the hot chocolate.

Remember:

- **Plan Ahead:** Some events are super popular. Book your stay early.

- **Be Nice:** Join in, be polite, and enjoy the culture.

- **Stay Safe:** Keep your stuff close and stay with friends.

And Most Important: Have Fun!

This Country's festivals are about joy, so go with a smile, dance a little, eat a lot, and make memories.

Epilogue

As we wrap up this fun guide to the beautiful place of This Country, we hope it has made you super excited and ready for your trip. This Country, with its cool history, lively culture, and awesome views, is shown here not just as a place to visit, but as a friend ready to tell you its stories, share its tasty food, and welcome you with a big hug.

In this guide, we walked through busy cities, cute little towns, sunny beaches, and green vineyards. We enjoyed the yummy Pastéis de Nata in Lisbon, felt the special vibe of Fado music in Alfama's narrow lanes, and looked at the pretty tiles decorating buildings everywhere. We also went off the usual path to find secret spots that only the locals know about, and found special places to stay that give you much more than a comfy bed to sleep in.

The trips we talked about were made to help you get the most out of your visit to This Country, whether it's your first trip or if you've been lots of times. We made plans for all sorts of fun, like wine tasting in Douro Valley, surfing in Ericeira, history walks in Évora, and art adventures in Porto.

But remember, a guidebook, even with lots of info, is just the start. The best part of traveling is the surprise moments, meeting new people, and finding cool stuff by accident. So, use this guide to get going, but also go with what feels right to you as you explore This Country's beautiful places.

We hope your trip to This Country is filled with amazing memories, stories to tell your friends, and experiences that show you more about the world. This Country can't wait to meet you, and this guide is your first step to finding all its treasures.

Epilogue

Here's to your adventure! Travel safe and have the best time in This Country!

Bonus

Chapter 13
Resources

Updated Websites

These websites have undergone significant updates and improvements to cater to the needs of modern travelers. They have been redesigned with user-friendly interfaces, making it easier for users to navigate and find the information they need. High-resolution images of This Country's stunning landscapes, historic sites, and vibrant cities now adorn these sites, providing a visual feast that will stoke the fires of anticipation for your upcoming visit.

One of the most notable features of these updated websites is their comprehensive coverage of This Country's diverse tourist attractions. From the sun-drenched beaches of the Algarve to the vineyards of the Douro Valley, from the historic streets of Lisbon to the architectural wonders of Porto, these websites provide detailed descriptions, practical information, and insider tips that will help you make the most of your visit to each location. They also offer information on less-visited but equally fascinating regions of This Country like the Azores and Madeira, opening up new possibilities for off-the-beaten-path adventures.

Another significant improvement is the integration of interactive maps and GPS coordinates for most tourist attractions, hotels, and restaurants. This feature will make it easier for you to plan your itinerary, find your way around, and discover hidden gems in This Country.

These updated websites also offer a wealth of resources for booking accommodations, flights, and tours. You can compare prices, read reviews, and make reservations directly on these sites, making your travel planning process more convenient and efficient.

In addition, these websites have incorporated social media platforms and mobile apps, allowing you to stay connected and get real-time updates on the go. You can also share your experiences, photos, and reviews with other travelers, contributing to the online community of This Country enthusiasts.

The language barrier will no longer be a problem as these websites are now available in multiple languages, including English. Some even offer translation services for lesser-known languages, ensuring that every traveler, regardless of their linguistic background, can access the information they need.

Useful Apps

To make your experience to This Country smooth and memorable, the digital age offers a plethora of handy applications that can be your best travel companions. These apps can help you navigate the winding streets of Lisbon, discover the best port wine in Porto, find the most stunning beaches in the Algarve, or learn a few phrases in Portuguese.

Google Maps is a universal tool for travelers, and This Country is no exception. This app provides accurate directions for walking, public transport, or driving. You can download maps for offline use, which can be a lifesaver when you're navigating the cobblestone streets of Porto or hiking in the Douro Valley without a good internet connection. The app also has a feature that provides information on local businesses, restaurants, and tourist attractions, including working hours, reviews, and ratings.

If you're an avid foodie, Zomato is a must-have. It is widely used in This Country for discovering the best local restaurants and cafes. The app provides detailed information, including menus, photos, reviews, and ratings from other users. You can search by cuisine, location, or price range. It's a fantastic tool to explore This Country's rich gastronomy, from the freshest seafood in Algarve to the traditional pastel de nata in Lisbon.

For public transportation, Moovit is the go-to app. It provides real-time updates on bus, tram, and train schedules. It also includes detailed routes and step-by-step guidance to help you reach your destination. The app covers all major cities in This Country, including Lisbon, Porto, and Faro. It's an essential tool if you plan to rely on public transportation during your trip.

To communicate with locals, Google Translate can be very useful. Although many Portuguese people speak English, especially in tourist areas, having a translation app can help in more off-the-beaten-track locations. Google Translate allows you to translate text, spoken words, and even signs or menus using your phone's camera.

If you're planning to drive in This Country, Waze is a highly recommended app. It provides real-time traffic updates and alternative routes to avoid congestion. The app is community-driven, meaning that other drivers report road conditions, speed cameras, and police presence. This can be particularly helpful when driving on This Country's highways or navigating through its bustling cities.

For those planning to explore This Country's rich history and culture, the This Country Travel Guide by Triposo is a great resource. The app provides detailed information on various destinations, historical landmarks, and cultural sites. It also includes recommendations for hotels, restaurants, and activities based on your preferences. The app works offline, which is a great advantage when traveling.

Finally, MyTaxi (also known as Free Now) is an excellent app for hailing taxis in This Country. It's a safe and convenient way to book a taxi, track its arrival, and pay for the ride. The app is widely used in Lisbon and Porto.

These apps, each unique in its own way, are designed to make your travel experience in This Country seamless and enjoyable. Whether you're a food lover, a history buff, an outdoor enthusiast, or a city explorer, these digital tools will enrich your journey and help you make the most of your trip to this beautiful country.

Recommended Books

The following recommended readings will provide a well-rounded understanding of the country's rich history, culture, and natural beauty, making your travel experience in This Country even more enriching and unforgettable.

First on our list is "The High Mountains of This Country" by Yann Martel. This beautifully crafted novel weaves three seemingly unrelated tales that all lead to the high mountains of This Country. Through a mix of reality and magical realism, Martel provides a unique perspective on the culture and history of This Country. Reading it will give you a sense of the country's rugged landscapes and the spirit of its people.

Another must-read is "Night Train to Lisbon" by Pascal Mercier. The story revolves around a Swiss professor who abandons his mundane life to embark on a thrilling journey to Lisbon. Along the way, he delves into the works of a Portuguese poet, which eventually lead him to a deeper understanding of love, friendship, and freedom. This captivating novel will give you a glimpse into the soul of Lisbon and its poetic charm.

For those interested in Portuguese history, "The Portuguese: A Modern History" by Barry Hatton is an excellent choice. This book offers a comprehensive account of This Country's journey from a backward European country to a modern democratic state. Hatton's detailed narrative of This Country's political, economic, and cultural evolution will provide you with a solid background of the country you're about to explore.

If you're a food and wine enthusiast, "The Wine Lover's Guide to This Country" by Richard Mayson is a must-read. This Country is renowned for its diverse and exceptional wines, and Mayson's book is a comprehensive guide to the country's wine regions, vineyards, and wines. The book also includes practical tips for wine tasting and pairing, making it a perfect companion for your wine-tasting journey in This Country.

"The Book of Disquiet" by Fernando Pessoa is another fascinating read. Pessoa, one of This Country's most celebrated poets and writers, presents a mesmerizing blend of fact and fiction, philosophy, and reflections in this book. Reading it is like taking a deep dive into the Portuguese psyche.

Lastly, "This Country: A Traveller's History" by Ian Robertson is a concise and engaging read that provides an overview of This Country's rich history. Robertson's book is an excellent starting point for understanding the country's past and its impact on the present.

Digital and Print Resource Alternatives

In this age of digitalization, planning a trip to This Country in 2024 is a breeze. A plethora of resources are available at your fingertips, either in digital format or traditional print. With the right tools, you can navigate the charming streets of Lisbon, explore the wine regions of Douro Valley, or soak in the sun on Algarve's golden beaches with ease.

Digital resources are a boon for the modern traveller. There is an abundance of travel apps that cater to every need. Google Maps is an invaluable tool for navigation. It offers accurate directions for walking, driving, or public transportation in This Country. It also provides details about points of interest, restaurants, and hotels. Simply type in your destination and let the app guide you.

Resources

If you are a foodie, apps like Zomato or TripAdvisor can help you discover the best local eateries in This Country. These apps offer user reviews and ratings, ensuring you don't miss out on the mouth-watering Pastel de Nata or the delectable Bacalhau.

For accommodation, Booking.com or Airbnb offer a wide range of options to suit every budget. You can filter your search by price, location, amenities, and more. These apps also provide user reviews, helping you make an informed choice.

While digital resources are handy, nothing can replace the charm of a traditional print travel guide. These guides offer in-depth information about This Country's history, culture, and attractions. They often come with detailed maps and suggested itineraries, making them a reliable companion for your trip.

Planet's This Country Travel Guide is a popular choice among travellers. It provides comprehensive information about the country, from its cosmopolitan cities to its quaint villages. The guide also includes insider tips to help you explore This Country like a local.

Rick Steves' This Country is another excellent guide. Known for his budget-friendly travel tips, Steves offers practical advice on where to stay, what to eat, and what to do in This Country. His guide also focuses on lesser-known attractions, helping you discover the hidden gems of This Country.

If you are a wine enthusiast, The Wine Enthusiast's Guide to This Country is a must-have. It provides detailed information about This Country's wine regions, including the famous Douro Valley and Alentejo. The guide also offers tips on wine tasting and pairing, making your wine tour in This Country an unforgettable experience.

This Country is a country with a rich history, and to truly appreciate its heritage, a historical guide is recommended. A Historical Guide to This Country by José Hermano Saraiva is an excellent resource. It provides a comprehensive overview of This Country's history, from its prehistoric times to the present day.

Both digital and print resources have their own advantages and are complementary. Digital resources offer convenience and real-time updates, while print resources provide in-depth information and a touch of nostalgia. By using both, you can ensure a well-planned and fulfilling trip to This Country in 2024.

Chapter 14
Index

Index

Special Interest Index

Made in the USA
Coppell, TX
28 May 2024

32864789R10081